OH, DEM GOLDEN SLIPPERS!

Arr. by F. LOUIS.

Words and Music by JAS. A. BLAND.

MODERATO.

1. Oh, my gold-en slippers am laid away, Kase I don't 'spect to wear 'em till my
2. Oh, my ole ban-jo hangs on de wall, Kase it aint been tuned since
3. So, it's good bye, children, I will have to go Whar de rain don't fall or de

weddin' day, And my long-tail'd coat, dat I loved so well, I will wear up in de chariot in de morn; And my
way last fall, But de darks all say we will hab a good time, When we ride up in de chariot in de morn; Dar's ole
wind don't blow, And yer uls-ter coats, why, yer will not need, When yer ride up in de chariot in de morn: But yer

J. F. P. & Co. 1413—3.

Copyright, 1879, by John F. Perry & Co.

Page 3.

OH! DEM GOLDEN SLIPPERS

The Mummers Parade is never complete without Indians. They provide an opportunity for elaborate and colorful costuming and a lavish display of plumes. Indian dances also provide a good basis for pageantry and drills. Here's a perfect combination of the traditions of the Old World and the New.

OH! DEM GOLDEN SLIPPERS

Charles E. Welch

THOMAS NELSON INC.   NEW YORK   CAMDEN

CONTENTS

For Elizabeth
who has seen so many Mummers Parades
and
for Megan
who never saw any

ACKNOWL-
EDGMENTS

Without the Mummers, there would be no Parade, and without the Parade there would be no book; therefore, my first debt of gratitude is owed to those men and women who participate in the Philadelphia Mummers Parade. Doing this book has given me a wonderful opportunity to talk to many of them. At all times I was met with courtesy and candor. The mistakes in this book are mine, most of the information is theirs.

Mr. Joseph A. Ferko, Mr. John Mooney, Sr., Mr. John Mooney, Jr., Mr. Thomas McCann, Mr. John Gilbert, Mr. John Baukus were especially helpful. Mr. David Nelson was a great aid in pulling together the facts about the birth of the String Bands.

Many professional folklorists were generous with their help. Among them were Dr. John Greenway, Dr. Kenneth Goldstein, Dr. Don. Yoder, Dr. Robert Byington, Dr. Daniel J. Crowley, Dr. Charles Seeger, and the late Dr. MacEdward Leech.

Mr. George Kearney encouraged me and led me in the early stages of this work. I have a special place in my affection for Miss Berjoohy Haigazian through whom I was led to the notebooks of Miss Evlyn Shuler where much original material was found.

The *Philadelphia Evening and Sunday Bulletin* and its librarian, Mr. Charles Martyn, were most cooperative. The Pennsylvania Historical Society and its leadership provided most of the diary material. The Philadelphia City Archives was the source of much of the legal material.

Special thanks also to Mr. Gregory Meyer, who furnished most of the photographs for the book.

Portions of this book, in a somewhat altered form were published in the *Journal of American Folklore,* the *Keystone Folklore Quarterly,* and the *Mummers Magazine.*

THE QUAKER MYTH

Every city has its cold, inanimate monuments of historic and cultural interest: old buildings, bronze statues, and great boulevards. Philadelphia has a living, breathing memorial to its greatness: the Mummers Parade. At the first of every year, there is a lilt in the air, a song on the town: princes and clowns, columbines and harlequins dance in the streets. Serpents and devils, angels and sinners, young and old—all blend into one massive, undulating bright-colored throng. Blue, red, and yellow capes; white satin daisies; plush-red roses; laughter and life cover the city. The sound comes before the sight—"Oh! Dem Golden Slippers," barely heard at first, swells as banjos and glockenspiels feed out of the narrow lively streets into Broad Street. They come out of the heart of Philadelphia, these unique "Shooters" in their stunning and incongruous magnificence, and the rest of Philadelphia—at least a million and a quarter people—stand to watch them: a Viking carrying a hundred square feet of costume, a Fancy Captain with a great train, uncountable clowns in indescribable array, a myriad of musicians—the work of a year expended on one day of glory.

The splendor of the past is lightened by the satire of the present: "General Charles de Gaulle" rests on the seventh day of his labors of creation; "Mary Poppins" drifts above a city seamier than London; "Tiny Tim" tiptoes through the tulips to his "Miss Vicki"; the Purul Comics clown around on the moon; "American Soldiers in Vietnam" are warmed by the burning of draft cards; a Murray Comic Club gladiator battles a smoke-billowing, air-polluting "dinosaur"; and the Hammond Club pays tribute to the late Walt Disney, while the Liberty Clowns dance the Strut with "Snoopy." The past year is held up to a fun-house wavy mirror, and its events deflated to their proper insignificance.

7

Inconspicuously rebellious, a few blackface clowns do their Strut in defiance of minority groups, majority groups, and all officialdom; the other clowns bow (as Mummers, with their curious bent-knee dance, can so easily do) to the latest decree of the authorities, and put aside the burnt cork for gold makeup—gold to daub the faces of willing and eager girls along the way and thus to lay the letter and the spirit of a past prohibition. Black for gold, gold for black; a golden lining for the blackface controversy of the past, and "Golden Slippers" yet once more in the streets of Philadelphia.

Dancing along with the golden slippers of the marchers parading up Philadelphia's Broad Street—"the longest, straightest street in the world," the city fathers claim—go many questions. What is the life story of this perennial? What is its reason for being? What chance has selected Philadelphia as the home of this magnificent spectacle—or is it chance? What really is going on in Philadelphia at the beginning of January every year?

In searching through the local papers, past and present, for the answers to these questions, one can easily establish a pattern. The papers are full of information concerning the Shooters and their spectacle from 1901 to the present, but there is no indication of their origin. The Parade has just grown like Topsy as far as the papers are concerned, and that is that. The only historical information is found in the Philadelphia *Public Ledger* of November 17 to 23, 1930, in the form of six essays. The author of this article, Frances Burke Brandt, who was a prominent local historian, made the first and, until now, the only attempt to establish the origins of the Philadelphia Parade.

Going through the early newspapers and diaries in the Quaker City searching for the seeds of mummery, one senses first of all a hostility toward the tendency to pageantry, and especially to the proleterian presentation. This hostility is a mystery until one studies traditions similar to the one in Philadelphia found abroad, especially those of Great Britain. The early customs in the City of Brotherly Love, at least those connected with mummery, resemble those found in Great Britain in connection with the Mummers' Play, the Plough Play, and the Sword Dance. From the earliest times of its presentation, probably in the fifteenth century, in

8

England, the Mummers' Play was performed by the less well-to-do. Tiddy in his *The Mummers' Play* says that he was never able to find any evidence that it was performed by the upper classes in a highly stratified society. This pattern continued in America. Daniel R. Gilbert in his unpublished "Patterns of Organization and Membership in Colonial Philadelphia Club Life, 1725-1753" points up the situation. In discussing Philadelphia social organizations, Dr. Gilbert considers all the "respectable" elements in the city, but ignores the laborers, apprentices, and servants who were "at the bottom of the economic and social scale," and "had yet to come to political or social expression." These were the very people who would be most likely to celebrate the Mummers' Play and those traditions surrounding it. Needless to say, there is no mention of Mummers in Dr. Gilbert's work.

The average Parade participant was most certainly not one to keep a diary or leave any account of his social activities. The major source of information about this social order is from outsiders —people who did keep diaries—and the public records, both providing only sketchy and insufficient accounts. Going over this material, one begins to realize that while it certainly indicates that the Parade derives from European celebrations, it is much more than simply a remnant. Cultural survivals have a way of taking on a life of their own when they are divorced from their original significance, and this is what has happened in Philadelphia. Through the years a fully developed personality of its own emerges, but before we can explore it thoroughly, we must examine its source. Why has this flower bloomed in the Quaker City? To answer this question with some degree of reliability, we must examine this country town at its beginning.

When the city of Philadelphia was incorporated, stern Quaker influence set its stamp upon it and directed the fledgling's future growth. The plan of the city was indicative of the Quaker energy and thought. Penn laid down specifics for the physical and moral welfare of his colonists. He instructed his agents to

be sure to make your choice where it is most navigable, high, dry, and healthy; that is where most ships best ride, of deepest draught of water, if possible to load or unload at the bank or keyside without boating or literage and saw that they followed his orders. He further instructed his representatives in the New World—a world he was yet to see—that "no vice or evil conversation go uncomplained of or unpunished in any way; that God be not provoked against the country."

William Penn sought settlers from the Continent as well as from his ancestral home, England. Germany and Holland sent many immigrants, most of whom were Quakers. The newcomers were offered 5,000 acres of land in Penn's Holy Experiment for 100 pounds cash; in addition there was to be an annual rental of a shilling for every 100 acres. Those who could not buy could rent land at an annual cost of one shilling for each acre. Many accepted the invitation and sailed forth to help fulfill Penn's dream of a city "which will never be burnt, and always wholesome." However, as we shall see, the dream was soon taken over by other than Quaker elements.

First of all Philadelphia, like its sister cities Newport, Boston, Charleston, and New York, was a port city and as such was in a constant state of change. One indication of this was the inordinate number of taverns. In this respect Philadelphia was in worse shape than any of her sister cities. By 1698 conditions were such that the authorities had to apologize for the brawls and tippling so much a part of this Quaker city. The fault was, they said, that Philadelphia had "become the rode where sailors and others doe frequently pass and repass between Virginia and New England." These rarely passed without stopping over in such popular taverns of the day as the White Horse and the Blue Anchor, where they spent their time in drinking, gambling, and wenching.

As early as 1685, despite strenuous efforts on the part of the city fathers, the community was scene to many debaucheries which seaport towns fell heir to because of "the number of sailors of every nationality, [and] of foreign merchants and tradesmen come to buy and sell." Contributing to this "lewdness and all manner of wickedness" were the presence of the caves—subterranean dwellings along the shore of the Delaware River—which Penn ordered cleared for "ye reputation of the Government."

To combat this state of near anarchy, the Provincial Council of Pennsylvania created a watch for Philadelphia, which soon enabled Penn to announce that "after nine at Night, Officers go the

Rounds, and no person without a very good cause [is] suffered to be at any Public House that is not a Lodger."

All of this was in a city primarily controlled by the Quakers who had, by 1685, created two meeting houses and a yearly meeting that had authority over Pennsylvania, West Jersey, and Delaware. Although the Society of Friends put forth no program for legally propagating their faith, a uniformity was established early—a uniformity which coped with crime and held the line at times, but at other times failed miserably. Even this nominal control was soon to go out of Quaker hands.

Secular culture seemed to dominate Philadelphia early, in part a result of the liberal attitude of the Friends. Penn, at the request of "Sundry Freemen and Inhabitants" who had asked for an act "strengthening and confirming the City Charter and enabling the Mayor and Commonalty to make Bylaws," granted a charter in 1701.

This charter helped, but evidently Philadelphians still were human and venal for, in 1703, four barbers were arrested for "trimming people on the first," and Quakers continue to deplore the apprentices and other young men for taking "licentious liberty in robbing of orchards especially on the first day."

Within a very short time after this, the Quaker legal influence waned, and the religious uniformity began to dissolve. From the first, all religions were welcomed in Philadelphia, which open-arms policy led the way for the entrance of new sects as early as the 1690s. In 1692 Presbyterians and Baptists shared a common house of worship in harmony. The Presbyterians in 1698 established a separate church which embraced English dissenters, Welshmen, and Huguenots. The Episcopalian missionary, Thomas Clayton, began his work in Philadelphia in 1705 at about the time the Philadelphia Presbytery was organized. The arrival of the Scotch-Irish in 1719 caused the Presbyterian faith to grow tremendously.

It was in the Episcopal Church, however, where the "better sort" found their place, and soon after 1700 the Governors, who were rarely Quakers, gathered around them these non-Quaker elements, which gradually took over the city government as well as its society. Some such were Dr. John Kearsley, the Biddles, Charles Read, and Peter Chevalier. Still holding some power, however, were such Quaker families as the Norrises, Shippens,

Pembertons, Dickensons, Hills, Merediths, and Fishbourns; but their power was on the wane.

Ethnic homogeneity soon followed the religious and political path to assimilation. The chief port of entry for Germans after 1717 was Philadelphia, and many of these immigrants remained in the area. Before many years Philadelphia became almost bilingual as there were nearly as many Germans as English.

The population of Philadelphia was 55,000 in 1793 when a new element was added: the French. As a result of unstable conditions in the Sugar Islands, the French were forced to flee to the New World in great numbers, and again Philadelphia the port city was the major target. The incoming French brought with them many more elements that helped to overcome Quaker influence, except as a moral force. French *joie de vivre* stormed the barricades. J. H. Powell in his *Bring Out Your Dead* has provided us with a good portrait of the French and Philadelphia:

> Philadelphia was a new and fresh experience for the refugees: so were they for Philadelphia. Their *insouciance,* their cleverness and occupations, their street games and songs, their ready adjustment, their avid participation in the cock fighting, rope dancing, gambling, taverns, theatres, and alehouses of Philadelphia contributed to give the city, in spite of the heat and draught, what the Reverend Henry C. Helmuth termed "a merry, sinful summer."

This, then, was the ground in which the seed of Mummer merriment was sown and flourished—a city founded by Quakers, but not a Quaker city.

SITTIN BEGGARS GUMNA SPEED

No one can say what the real beginning of the Philadelphia Mummers Parade was, but possibly the Swedes started the Mummers Parade in the Swedish "Neck" of South Philadelphia not long after Penn laid out his squared green city. This supposition is supported by some evidence: the practice of certain early Mummers of visiting from house to house, and the shooting off of guns in connection with these visits.

In Sweden the celebration on the eve of St. John (St. Hans), June 24, is observed by general visiting and parties. Great bonfires are built and fed with nine different sorts of wood. Into this fire is thrown a kind of toadstool which is supposed to frighten off evil spirits. Another aspect of this holiday is the discharging of firearms.

The practice of visiting is also found in Sweden in connection with the celebration of the Santa Lucia festival, December 13. The celebration starts with a young girl, wearing a crown of six or seven lighted candles, entering the room and singing the hymn in praise of Saint Lucy, the Saint of Light. An entourage of young girls carrying lighted candles follows; then, bringing up the rear, come the Star Boys. These youths, dressed in long white robes and crowns, carry rods topped with stars. At the finish of the procession they visit other houses in the community collecting gifts of money or cakes.

Dr. Francis B. Brandt tells of reading in the memoirs of Henry Melchoir Muhlenberg (1711-1787) an account of a meeting with a 13 band of these early Swedish settlers on the roads in the Tinicum and Kingsessing portions of the "Neck," celebrating the New Year disguised as clowns "shouting at the top of their voices and shooting guns."

Other national groups seem to have made their contributions too. With the further development of the English settlement in Philadelphia, the English, too, celebrated the turn of the year. It was among these early pioneer families, as well as among the Germans and the Scotch-Irish, that the original Mummers were found.

The Scotch-Irish brought a tradition from northeastern Scotland of going from house to house on New Year's, singing this song or a similar one:

> The Guide new year it is begun,
> B'soothan, b'soothan
> The beggars they're begun to run,
> An awa b'mony a toon.
> Rise up goodwife, and dinna be sweer,
> B'soothan, b'soothan,
> An deal yir chirity t'the peer,
> An awa b'mony a toon.
> May your bairnies n'er be peer,
> B'soothan, b'soothan,
> Nor yet yir coo misgae the steer,
> An away b'mony a toon.
> It's nae for oorsels it we come here,
> B'soothan, b'soothan,
> It's for.................... sae scant o'gear,
> An awa b'mony a toon.
> We sing for meal, we sing for maut,
> B'soothan, b'soothan,
> We sing for cheese an a'thing fat,
> An awa b'mony a toon.
> Fess naither cog nor yet the mutty,
> B'soothan, b'soothan,
> Bit fess the peck fou' lairge and lucky,
> An awa b'mony a toon.
> The roods are slippery, we canna rin,
> B'soothan, b'soothan,
> We maun myne oor feet for fear we fa,
> An rin b'mony a toon.

At the end of the song a question was put: "Are you gueede for beggars?" "Sometimes," countered the householder. "Fah are ya beggin for?" "For so-and-so." If the person named was worthy, the alms were given and received with thanks usually in the form of doggerel.

When the young men were asked to sit down and partake of the New Year's food, they would refuse with "Na, na, sittin beggars cumma speed." With that the whisky and, for less robust souls, ale was brought out; then the thiggars drank up and were on their way. This custom was called "thigging" (begging) in Scotland.

A similar pattern is found in Staffordshire; here the visitors are called *guisers* and perform a play for their dole. This play was still acted every Christmas as late as 1886, according to local records. It opens with an appeal,

> Open-the-door: I open the door as I come in,
>   Hoping your favour for to win;
> Whether I rise, or stand, or fall,
>   I do my duty to please you all
> A room, a room, brave British, room! and give
>   me room to rise (read tide).

Open-the-door then calls in Sing Ghiles, who is followed immediately by King George. A duel ensues. Just as King George is about to win, a soldier, Bold Slasher, enters; after much conversation, the king and soldier clash. The soldier is wounded, and Open-the-door calls for the Doctor who revives the Bold Slasher. No sooner has the Slasher recovered, when the Black Prince enters, and challenges King George. They clash, and are interrupted by Open-the-door with this speech:

> Put up them swords and be at rest,
> For peace and quietness is the best.
> Enter in old Beelzebub.

After Beelzebub's entering speech, the Chorus sings this song:

> I am a jovial tinker,
>   I've travelled both far and near,
> And I never did meet with a singer
> Without he could drink some beer.
> We can either eat or drink,
>   Whilst the bells of England tingle;

15

But if you will give me your chink,
   I'll make the ladle jingle.
So I come meddle, come mend your kettle,
   I want to make you crazy;
Come double your money and thrible your money,
   I want to make you easy.

Then comes the plea for money or other gifts:

Open-the-door: Enter in Little Jack Dout!

Jack Dout (*with a broom, sweeping*).

Here comes Little Jack Dout,
With my brush I'll sweep you all out;
Money I want and money I crave,
Or else I'll sweep you all into your grave.

Now ladies and gentlemen, you that are able,
Put your hands in your pockets and remember the ladle,
For when I am dead and in my grave
No more of the ladle I shall crave.

A collection is taken up, and a song is rendered by the entire company, after which they march off "to the sound of the merry horn."

A similar custom takes place in Staffordshire, Cheshire, and North Shropshire on November 1 (All Saints Day) or on October 31 (the Eve of All Souls). Here the custom is called "souling" and is practiced almost entirely by children. They go from house to house begging for cakes, apples, or ale and singing the following songs:

Soul, soul, for an apple!
Pray, good missie, a couple!
One for Peter, two for Paul
And three for Him as made us all!
Allaby, allaby, eeby ee!
Christmas comes but once a year,
When It's gone It's never the near.
For goodness sake,
A soul cake!

Because live animals are forbidden, these bullfighters had to leave their bulls at home.

In every parade there
are always clowns.

Up with your kettle and down with your pan,
Give me an apple and I'll be gone!

The cock sat up in the yew-tree,
    The hen came chackling by,
I wish you all good morning,
    And a good fat pig in the sty.
    A good fat pig in the sty!

The lanes are very dirty,
    My shoes are very thin,
I pray good missis and master
    To drop a penny in!
    To drop a penny in!

Here comes one, two, three, jolly boys,
    All in a mind.
We are come a souling
    For what we can find,
Both ale, beer, and brandy,
    And all sorts of wine.
        (*Would ye be so kind, would ye be so kind?*)
We'll have a jug of your (best old March) beer,
And we'll come no more souling
    Till this time next year.
With walking and talking
    We get very dry,
I hope you good neighbours
    Will never deny.
Put your hand in your pocket,
    And pull out your keys,
Go down in your cellar
    And draw what you please.

                    ECCLESHALL, 1884

Soul, soul! for an apple or two!
If you've got no apples, pears'll do.
Up with your kettles and down with your pans,
Pray, good missis, a soul-cake!
Peter stands at younder gate,
Waiting for a soul-cake.
One for Peter, two for Paul,
Three for them that made us.
Souling-day comes once a-year,
That's the reason we come here.

                    KEELE, 1880

SITTIN
BEGGARS
CUMNA
SPEED

17

The English had their Mummers' Play, also known as the St. George Play.

The Mummers' Play, underdeveloped and episodic in its presentation, is found throughout England, Wales, and Scotland. Essentially the structure is that of a melodrama, with the cure generally used for comic relief. The Play opens with a presentation speech wherein an actor introduces the various participants. The first actor is usually St. George, who introduces himself with a bombastic speech. Then enters the Bold Slasher, the Turkish Knight, or another antagonist, and a dispute occurs. The two knights battle, and in most versions St. George wins.

Then comes the call for the Doctor, who, after much negotiation, brings the defeated antagonist back to life. Various comic characters, who next appear, usually have distinctive names (Big Head, Beelzebub, Johnny Jack, Devil Dout), and dance and sing, finishing the performance with a *quete* (collection) from the audience. A typical speech was:

> In come I, Little Devil Dout;
> If you don't give me money, I'll sweep you out.
> Money I want, money I crave;
> If you don't give me money,
> I'll sweep you to the grave.

After the collection, the group would move on to another house and repeat the play, freely changing the words and the action. Chambers has located over a hundred versions of this play.

This ceremony, usually presented over the Christmas season, has many interesting connections with other types of folk drama. Tiddy feels that:

> To consider the Mummers' Play in isolation and apart from the Sword Dance would be unsuitable and misleading, because in both these forms there is a combat, a death, and a revival, and this common feature is so essential that both forms must be attributed to common origin. In the Mummers' Play the dancing has dwindled to a very slight exercise, often to nothing more than characters walking round in circles.

Chambers has also noted the resemblance:

But the Mummers' Play, the Plough Play, and the Sword Dance, at least, are closely linked by common features: by attachment to the festivals of the rustic calendar, to Christmas or the resumption of agricultural work which follows upon Christmas, or to Easter; by the inevitable *quete* or 'gathering'; by the omnipresent fool; by the Man-Woman, that unquiet spirit for whom there is no obvious function, but for whom a place always has to be found; above all by the persistent theme of the Mock Death and the cure which is its almost invariable sequel.

Chambers has traced the St. George Play to an Elizabethan hack writer, Richard Johnson, who gathered traditional material under the title of *The Seven Champions of Christendom* published in 1596. Violet Alford, however, disagrees and puts an earlier date to the origin of this folk drama—1408.

The Scotch-Irish, in addition to their being the source of the speech, could have made another contribution—in the form of an especially interesting practice of their *guisers* that has much in common with the practices of the early Philadelphia paraders.

R. Chambers, *Book of Days,* gives a description of mummers together with an illustration of a group, showing various masks, and one character with the dragon's head. The Scottish *guisers,* referred to in the same work, are masked and each attended by a man in woman's clothing (the "Bessy"). They go from house to house on Hogmanay night (New Year's Eve) and sing or perform a play not unlike that of the English mummers.

Whatever the validity of priority of the preceding claimants, the major influence in the early days appears to have been the English folk play, the only survivals of which are some presentation verses and speeches that seem to stem from the English Mummers' Play, a seasonal ceremony with many interesting connections with other types of folk drama.

As we have seen, this performance is basically a melodrama and falls into four parts: the presentation; the battle or battles; the revival (i.e., bringing the losing warrior back to life through the ministrations of a "doctor") characterized by the "Call for the Doctor"; and the collection (from the spectators) of money or gifts of food and drink. This spectacle has not been found among the upper classes, which accounts in part for the lack of first-hand information gathered from participants.

The sources then, we see, of Philadelphia's present celebration of the New Year stretch back in many directions. As Philadelphia was the great "melting pot" long before New York and Boston welcomed immigrants from many lands, it is appropriate that it even now reflects this diversity of origin.

Here is an amalgam of similar customs of dissimilar backgrounds. The customs themselves are universal. Indeed New Year's visiting and "shooting" can be equated to folk practices in China, Japan, and the Slavic Lands long before there was any contact between the peoples of those places. Perhaps the persistence of the Mummers in Philadelphia can testify to this. Each new wave of newcomers—even to the present—finds in the parade a rekindling of a spark not at all nationalistic or regional—but a deep-seated human need to laugh at the past, to turn away from it and to greet the future with a sense of rebirth, a "turning of the new leaf," a need to play, to smile, to dance, and to hope for the brighter days to come.

COMMON NUISANCES

The current social scene is now being well preserved for those that follow us. The grand dinners, the debutante parties, the charity balls, are well documented for the generations that follow, if they care. The activities of the man in the street, however, are still often ignored and will be a matter of mystery in a century or two. So it has always been.

In Philadelphia, for example, a half hour's research will reveal the menu of the Assembly Ball held in 1898, but it would take half a lifetime to dig out the references to the Mummers Parade. Usually not a diary-keeper himself, the common man's activities are much more difficult to reconstruct than those of the upper classes who generally have among their members or families diary-keepers or letter-writers and letter-savers. As an elusive Mummer participant kept little of his life on personal record, we must go to the diaries of the upper classes and to the public records for any indication of his activities. The first clue is found in a 1702 Philadelphia grand-jury presentment, where we find mention of one John Smith, a resident of Strawberry Alley, presented for

> . . .being maskt or disguised in women's apparel; stalking openly
> through the streets of this city from house to house on or about
> the 26th of the 10 month [day after Christmas; under the Old
> Style calendar, December was the tenth month], it being against
> the Law of God, the law of this province and the law of nature,
> to the staining of holy profession and incoridigine of wickedness
> in this place.

All this for practicing the custom of Christmas mumming! Nor was this an exception, nor were men the only ones punished.

In the same document there is a report of Dorothy Canterill, presented for Christmas mumming and "walking and dancing in the house of John Simes at 9 to 10 o'clock at night." Sarah Stiner, charged with the same offense, was another victim of the prejudice against mumming. John Simes, in whose house the masquerade was held, was presented for keeping "a nursery to Dobotch ye inhabitants and youth of this city. . .to ye Greef of and disturbance of peaceable minds and propigating ye Throne of wickedness amongst us."

Could it be that John Smith, resident of Strawberry Alley, was presented for playing the "Bessy" of the English Mummers' Play? This is certainly a possibility. However, the arrest of those doughty females Dorothy Canterill and Sarah Stiner for masquerading as males indicates that this was general Christmas mumming, and not the English Mummers' Play. This is, nevertheless, the earliest example we have of people being punished for masking in the City of Brotherly Love.

The earliest diary comment yet to be found is that of Christopher Marshall: "1781—January 1—Firing guns in the night, before day sundry kinds of music, I presume, paraded the Streets, as they came our way."

We have a more complete account of the custom of mumming in Boston, given to us by Samuel Breck in his *Recollections:*

> They have ceased to do it now, but I remember them as late as 1782. They were a set of the lowest blackguards, who, disguised in filthy clothes and oft-time with masked faces, went from house to house in large companies. . . . One of them would cry out, "Ladies and Gentlemen sitting by the fire, put your hands in your pockets and give us our desire? . . .A kind of acting took place. One fellow was knocked down, and lay sprawling on the carpet, while another bellowed out,
>
> > "See, there he lies,
> > But ere he dies
> > A doctor must be had."
>
> He calls for a doctor, who soon appears, and enacts the part so well that the wounded man revives.

This is an obvious version of the English Mummers' Play, with its universal "Call for the Doctor." However, nothing comparable has been found in Philadelphia. One Philadelphia presentation rhyme has two lines in it which have been found in many presentation speeches in the English Mummers' Play. These two lines are:

> "Room! Room! my brave and gallant boys and girls
> give us room to rhyme."

Following these two lines, the leader continues:

> . . .and we will show you our slightest activity upon a New Years time. We also have taken the liberty to come here to remember you from year to year. God has spared us one year more that we may come into your door. We will eat and drink with all good cheer that we may live another year. Now I will conclude my speech as I have nothing more to say so get back boys and fire away.

At the end of the speech the "Band plays and march in house, get refreshments, dance for about a half-hour or until another company comes then a fight or get out." This description comes from a paper in the possession of a Mummer who dated it in 1930 as of "about 50 years ago or more." This dating puts the custom back to the early 80s or late 70s of the post-Civil War period where it undoubtedly was a carry-over from an earlier period. It appears from the ending that no play was presented, but that a half-hour of dancing was indulged in. What kind of dancing this was we do not know; however, it seems to have replaced the presentation of the English Mummers' Play.

Entries in early Philadelphia diaries make constant reference to the shooting off of guns in celebration of the New Year. This could be the source of the name by which the paraders are best known—Shooters. The term "New Year's Shooting" is still used by most of the present-day paraders; "Mummers" was the name given them by outsiders, for the custom of celebrating the New Year with shooting was not popular with the diary-keeping Philadelphians. Their attitude can be seen in a brief quotation from the Journal of a Quaker lady: "1793—Dec. 31. They are now practicing the foolish custom of firing out the old year; may the next be

23

spent to good purpose by those who are spared to see the end of it."

This early resentment of mumming and shooting of guns made fertile ground for the further restricting of masquerades and masked balls. This feeling and the general unrest caused by the political crisis that soon erupted into the Embargo Acts of January 9 and March 12, 1808, led to a resentment of all things foreign. The residents of Philadelphia had taken up the foreign custom of masked balls as early as 1800; they were well advertised and well attended at this time. However, times change and people present new problems. The beginning of the first great setback to the custom of mumming was triggered by the following advertisement in the Philadelphia *General Aurora Advertiser* for Thursday, January 28, 1808.

Subscription
for the
Masquerade Balls

Mr. Epervil, has the honor to inform the ladies and gentlemen of this city, that in consequence of an earnest invitation from a numerous circle of genteel and friendly persons, he has been induced to give three Masquerade Balls in this city; having previously taken all the necessary precautions to insure an agreeable, decent and select assembly.

Mr. E. will undertake to carry to the ladies of the subscribers, and will be particularly careful to remit to themselves, the tickets which they may desire, as soon as he receives notice.

Mr. E. being a musician will compose sundry pieces of music adapted to the different masked characters, and undertakes to select the most brilliant band of musicians that has been in this town, he will also have the pleasure to cause his orchestra to execute a variety of cotillions in full band as they are played in the opera at Paris.

Mr. E. flatters himself, that he shall neglect none of his best exertions to promote good order, decency and elegance.

Subscriptions will be opened for three Masquerade Balls, at 6 dollars, one half payable on subscribing—and the remaining half previous to the second ball.

Mr. E. expects to receive very soon, a general assortment of beautiful masks.

The first ball to be given in a fortnight.

The number of subscribers is fixed at 250.

Subscriptions to be had of Mr. E. No. 127 Spruce Street, corner of 5th, from 10 to 1 o'clock.

The religious leaders of the community rose in righteous wrath and moved to prevent the further practice of masquerading in Philadelphia. The first sign of this effort was to be seen in the *General Aurora Advertiser* for February 4, 1808, in a succinct advertisement from the pen of Monsieur Epervil:

Second & Last
Masquerade Ball
at the
Shakespeare Hotel
Corner of Sixth and Chestnut St.

Just at this time a French fleet anchored in the Delaware, and a wave of fear, tempered by anti-French feelings, contributed to the general feeling against mumming and masquerading. Sensing the consensus of the people, John Sergeant, a Federalist politician, eventually to be elected to Congress on that party's ticket, moved for the abolition of masked balls and masquerades. This resolution he presented to the House of Representatives of Pennsylvania, declaring that the tendency of masquerading was demoralizing.

The bill was rushed through both houses, and on February 15, 1808, the Act of February 15, 1808 (P.L. 49). Chapter XXXI, "An Act to Declare Masquerades and Masqued Balls to be Common Nuisances, and to Punish Those Who Promote Them" was passed. Section I of this act stated:

Be it enacted by the Senate and House of Representatives of the Commonwealth of Pennsylvania, in General Assembly met, and it is hereby enacted by the authority of the same, That masquerades and masqued balls, be, and they are hereby declared to be common nuisances; and every housekeeper within this commonwealth, who shall knowingly permit or suffer a masquerade or masqued ball to be held or given in his or her house, and every person who shall set on foot, promote or encourage, any masquerade or masqued ball, and every person who shall know-

25

ingly attend or be present at any masquerade or masqued ball, in mask, or otherwise, being thereof legally convicted, in the mayor's court of the city of Philadelphia, or in any court of quarter-sessions of the peace, or oyer and terminer and general goal delivery, shall, for each and every such offense, be sentenced to an imprisonment not exceeding three months, and to pay a fine not exceeding one thousand nor less than fifty dollars, and to give security in such sum as the court may direct, to keep the peace and be of good behaviour for one year.

And so the clock was turned back to the early days when mumming was called the agent in propagating wickedness. The mask was feared and mumming was identified with the mask and the fear; hence, the custom of mumming was held with its companion the masked ball as responsible for assaulting "the peace and dignity" of Pennsylvania, and was thrust from the bosom of the staid Commonwealth.

An interesting parallel to this may be found in the history of New Orleans, certainly more French than Philadelphia, where the Mardi Gras was outlawed in 1806. There were several reasons for this action, among which was a report that Aaron Burr was on his way down the Mississippi River to capture New Orleans. Burr did not get past Natchez, but the Mardi Gras was not revived for many years. Robert Tallant in his *Mardi Gras* describes this period:

> This time Mardi Gras almost died, and for years it existed only in the memory of the Creole population. In 1823, after numerous petitions, balls were at last, although begrudgingly, allowed once again, and in 1827 street-masking was once more permitted.

To Pennsylvanians there is still a stronger connection with the Mardi Gras, as may be seen from the following quotation from Tallant concerning the first major parade after the Mardi Gras was reinstated in 1827:

> A young man named Michael Krafft, who had been born in Pennsylvania and who had nothing that was Latin in him, had organized the Cowbellion de Rakin Society in Mobile in 1831. It was this organization which first paraded with torch and float, although in Mobile the pageants appeared on New Year's Eve. (Not until 1866 did Mobile have parades on Mardi Gras.) The

entire conception of the parades of the Cowbellions and of those later to become popular in New Orleans seems to have originated in the minds of Krafft and a few of his friends.

Masquerades, and by association, the custom of mumming, were outlawed until 1859, but a complete perusal of the Records of the Quarter Sessions Court, and a partial examination of the documents of the Mayor's Court covering this period reveals no convictions under this act. In addition, a thorough examination of the Daily Occurrences Dockets from 1808 to 1859 of the Walnut Street Prison shows no arrests for masquerading. In the Records of the Quarter Sessions Court when someone was tried for being or maintaining a "common nuisance," the nuisance was usually keeping a vicious dog. Even though there are no records to be found of arrests or convictions of people being apprehended for masquerading and mumming, it is safe to assume that, human nature being what it is, the custom continued although it was somewhat restricted.

We have one account of mumming during this period. In an interview published in January 1, 1937, in *The Evening Bulletin*, William H. Field, who was then 96 years old, reported on stories told him by his father. These stories place the date of the Parade as we know it as 1812. David Dudley Field, the father, had told his son that the first parade of Shooters started as the result of a quasi-military organization of men too young to be drafted into service for the War of 1812. Called Jackson's Rangers, they served as a kind of home guard providing their own equipment. These young men celebrated the New Year by mounting on black horses and visiting from house to house. At each house they would knock on the door, and when the occupant would come out they would recite a rhyme. From memory Mr. Field recited these rhymes as told him by his father:

> With sweet and loud music we now begin,
> We'll shoot the old year out and the
> new one in. . .

> He did look so droll
> With a quart of strawberries spread on
> his nose. . .

27

Here I stand before your door
As we have done the year before
Set your bottles on the shelves
We have whiskey enough to help
  ourselves.

Mr. Field's nephew, William R. Field, during this same interview recalled that the early Mummers smeared their faces with redwash, burnt cork, and flour. Wearing old and comic clothes they went from house to house in the "Neck," visiting and performing. Mr. Field contributed this speech as one typical of the early days:

We take liberty to come on your land
With guns and pistols in our hand;
We have shot and played for those who
  have let us in,
With string and brass band music we
  begin.
Don't get excited or amazed
When you see our powder blaze.
With shooting and music that we all
  admire,
What don't snap shall surely fire.

While Mr. William H. Field's version of the origin of the Mummers Parade is wrong—we have seen that people were parading and masking in Philadelphia long before 1812—he does give us a picture of mumming during the period in which it was banned as "a common nuisance."

The newspapers covering the time of the law reveal no specific instances of mumming, but they do report "great turnouts" and the air of "a festival" which gripped the city on New Year's Day. Military parades were not uncommon on this day as well as the general custom of visiting. *The United States Gazette* for January 2, 1839, reports on a military parade on January 1, 1839:

28

Yesterday the troops of the first (the city) Brigade paraded. We did not see the whole, but Col. Child's and Cap. Cadwallader's companies of Grays we saw marching to the place for forming the line.

Nor were the civilians entirely shut out:

Saturday evening was celebrated in the neighborhood of the city, with the usual demonstration of respect for the parting and coming year. Little men and great boys burnt powder, and kept up a regular "popping" out of doors. . . .

The "burning of powder" by the residents of Philadelphia seems to have been pretty well ignored by the city officials, for there is only one entry in the Daily Occurrences Docket of the Walnut Street Prison of a person being arrested for practicing this custom during the period from 1808 to 1859. The man arrested was a colored man, and one wonders how much his color had to do with his arrest, and how much the discharging of the gun. The entry reads "January 1, 1821. Philip State: (B) sentenced to 5 days for firing a gun." On this same day and on the same docket another man was given an equal sentence for swearing, so we are given some idea of the degree of this offense of shooting off a gun to greet the New Year. However, there are many newspaper items attesting to the fact that this custom was a dangerous one, and many young men were injured in their greeting to the New Year. Perhaps the frequency of these injuries caused the city officials to view this practice with more severity, for the *North American and United States Gazette* reports the following news item on January 3, 1848:

> Firing off the Old Year—Two individuals were fined, on Saturday, by the Major of the city, and one by the Mayor of the Northern Liberties for discharging fire arms on New Year's eve.

The Anti-Masquerade Act did not prevent Philadelphians from parading, and in the first part of the nineteenth century there were many great "turnouts." One such was in honor of the centennial of George Washington's birth, and was reported by the editor of the *North American and United States Gazette* on February 23, 1832:

> It remained for Chestnut Street, however, to present the most exhilarating spectacle. . . .The blooming flush of life and beauty brightening from the upper to the lower windows of every dwelling as far as the vision might extend; the glittering sails of the ship carried in the procession; the universal shout, ever and anon, from the unlimited crowd; the military appearing from afar

29

with their bristling bayonets and plumes, and their fine music, melting in Dorian mode from the distance—altogether formed a pomp and spell such as we do not expect soon to see or feel again.

General Lafayette, on his visit to Philadelphia in 1824, was met by 6,000 troops under General Cadwallader and was led on a grand tour of the city. Following the military display, the tradesmen of the town paraded with their trade and business floats. *Poulson's American Daily Advertiser* of September 30, 1824, reports that the most popular float was the one presented by the printers. This is described as bearing a legend: "Liberty of the Press: the surest guarantee of the rights of man."

The Fourth of July was always celebrated with appropriate parades and celebrations, so it is certain that Philadelphians had a sufficient number of parades for their amusement; and if they were not satisfied with these they could always go out of town. The custom of mumming moved into the outlying provinces during this period—or perhaps had been there all the time, and had not been banned. The following item from the *Easton Sentinel* of January 10, 1834, describes a New Year's Day parade:

The Fantasticals. On New Year's day our borough witnessed a parade of the fantasticals—the immediate body guard of the lately elected redoubtable Col. Sheffler. It was a new and perhaps an improved edition of the late parades in New York and Philadelphia. The corps including music (numbered) about one hundred. The Calithumpian band had been uniformed and pressed into service. These commenced their melody at about 10 o'clock in the forenoon and made the circuit of the town, playing the most splendid and novel voluntaries and variations. Their dresses displayed taste and ingenuity. All the quarters of the earth appeared to have been ransacked to swell the ranks of this Enterprian band. Indians, negroes, hunters, Falstaffs, Jim Crows and nondescripts, all displaying surprizing skill upon their several instruments, and with the most praiseworthy independence every man played his own tune—if he knew one; the greater number however gave voluntaries. Conch-shells, old cracked instruments, stones, shingles, tin-horns, speaking trumpets, here and there a bassoon, old kettles, pot-lids, dozens of cow-bells strung upon poles and iron hoops constituted their musical instruments. One had a leg covered with feathers, another had one of his understandings compressed into the smallest imaginable space, while its fellow was stuffed out to the dimensions of a moderate sized watchbox. It was high treason for any man's leg to look like its fellow; whiskers of all materials, and many of the size of an ordinary currant bush graced the masks or painted faces of the heroes. At about 11 o'clock the Colonel and an aid marched the corps in front of the band, who were stationed in the square. Upon the appearance of their commander such of the musicians as could do so without danger to their habiliments, saluted him by going down upon their knees. The Captain of the band wore a chapeau which was calculated and no doubt intended, in case of bad weather to serve as a tent for the whole corps.

The Colonel was mounted upon a Jackass, and the aid upon a black pony, which had the fodder for both tied to his tail. Their spurs were of tin of enormous size and of the latest and most approved construction, with swords to match. The provisions of the corps, consisting of mackerel, herring, beef-bones, &c. were generally carried upon the back or around the neck. Their field-piece was an acqueduct pipe mounted upon wheels, and fitted up in a corresponding style. One man in lieu of a musket sported a venison skin which had been polished by the guests of the Shakespeare; and another carried a tin musket and bayonet with which he might have picked a hole in a thunder cloud. If we remembered and wrote by steam, we perhaps would be able to give a detailed account of the dress, caps, mottoes, &c. as it is, we despair. One cap we remember ran up to a peak that rivalled the Peak of Teneriffe and could boast what the latter cannot—a weather-cock upon the top of it. One (a loyal fellow no doubt) carried a placard upon his back with a correct likeness of the Colonel and the motto, 'I'm de feller what can beat de lawyers.'

The above description gives us a good idea of what the early Philadelphia Mummers must have been like; in addition, we are given some indication that the Parade was no longer performed in Philadelphia.

In examining the material concerning the custom of mumming and parading on New Year's Day and the week after Christmas, and its relation to the material concerning the Anti-Masquerade Act, several points can be made. This custom was prevalent in the early days of the Colony, and from those earliest days was not popular with the more sedate members of the community. This unpopularity led to the eventual banning of the custom, but the ban was not severe and was not always obeyed or enforced.

The important thing to keep in mind is that this mumming was practiced by the ordinary citizens, who made up the majority of the population. As the population of the city grew, this law became even more difficult to enforce, and at no time during its fifty-year tenure was there any concerted effort to enforce it.

This custom remained alive, and in fact grew, for local legend has it that the first known club to be formed among the people for the purpose of parading was organized during this period. This club was called the Chain Gang, and was formed about 1846. However, nothing else is known about it. It did exist, though, and did parade throughout the South Philadelphia area. There are still some men living whose fathers remembered this organization and told them of it.

If any answer can be given to the importance of the banning of the custom of Christmas mumming and masquerading, it would lie in the analysis of the question: Why was this law not enforced? There is every evidence that it was almost totally ignored. To mention only the fact that no arrests are listed for this offense in the Daily Occurrences Dockets of the Walnut Street Prison from 1808 to 1859, would be sufficient evidence on which to base an opinion. However, this evidence, coupled with the lack of trials in the Mayor's Court and the Quarter Sessions Court, and the dearth of newspaper material concerning arrests for violations of the Anti-Masquerade Act give us ample evidence that this law was not enforced. Why?

One answer to this question is that the law was made by the leaders of the community, not the followers. The aristocracy was more in control in the passing of laws than in the enforcing of them. At this time in the city's history the system of constable enforcement was used. In 1811 there were fourteen constables, one for each ward, and one high constable. These constables were required to go about the city and to examine all vagrant and disorderly persons and, if they were not satisfied by their examination, they were charged to bring suspicious people before the mayor or an alderman. In addition, these officers of the law had to light the lamps in the city. In the early days of the Anti-Masquerade Act there were too few constables, and too many disturbances for them to cope with. They did not have the time or energy to check on the custom of mumming. It is significant that the law was more successful in controlling masked balls than it was in stopping the custom of mumming. The aristocrats, who patronized the masked balls, were more amenable to suggestion, and they were more in the eye of public officials, and so were more easily observed. Hence, there are no records of masked balls being held, but many indications that the custom of mumming continued.

Seemingly the law and the lawbreakers were just not important enough to regulate closely. In addition, the constables were elected by the people, and many more voters were from the lower class than from the upper class. The constables, undoubtedly aware that interference with the people on small issues could cause unnecessary troubles, apparently adopted a hands-off policy. As we have seen, the Chain Gang Mummer organization was formed during this ban, and soon other groups were organized, causing a change in public opinion, and forcing the repeal of the Anti-Masquerade Act in 1859.

Another source of information on the pre-Civil War period of the Parade is to be found in Scharf and Westcott, one of the thorough Philadelphia histories, which gives this account, documented by an anonymous "informant."

> It was considered the proper thing in those days to give the leading mummers a few pence as a dole, which in the language of the present time they would pool, and buy cakes and beer. It was also regarded as the right thing to do to invite them into the house and regale them with mulled cider, or small beer, and homemade cakes. It was considered a great breach of etiquette to address or otherwise recognize the mummer by any other than the name of the character he was assuming. I remember a little girl who, with all the curiosity of her sex, had discovered a neighbor's boy in the party, and with childish impetuosity she broke out with, "Oh, I know thee, Isaac Simmons. Thee is not George Washington."

Scharf and Westcott also give us some examples of early presentation speeches:

33

> Here comes I, old Beelzebub,
> On my shoulder I carry a club,
> In my hand a dripping pan—
> Don't you think I'm a jolly old man?

In one version in Scharf and Westcott "a frying pan" is substituted for "a dripping pan" and in another, Little Devil Dout is replaced by Cooney Cracker:

> Here comes I, old Cooney Cracker!
> I swear to God my wife chews terbacker!
> A pipe is good; cigars are better;
> When I get married I'll send you a letter.

A variant of this presentation differs in the three last lines:

> I want some money to buy tobacco;
> Tobacco's good; cigars are better
> Give me some money, or I'll marry your daughter.

Finally, the most interesting of all speeches indicates that the early Mummers substituted George the President for George the Saint:

> Here am I, great Washington!
> On my shoulders I carry a gun. . . .

No more is given on the above verse, except the comment that this is all that is remembered; however, one further reference in the limited literature on the Philadelphia Mummers Parade is given by Dr. Francis Burke Brandt in a popularized article that appeared in a local Philadelphia paper. Dr. Brandt asserts that at one time several verses were used by the Mummer impersonating Washington, and that Washington enjoyed them so much that he had his aide copy the many versions down.

The Philadelphia Mummers Parade as we know it today really began after the Civil War. The early history is speculative and sketchy, but its post-Civil War history can be traced from much more definitive information, for the parades were covered fully in the papers and there is some limited manuscript material available.

HERE WE STAND BEFORE YOUR DOOR

The nineteenth century was a personal one; during the last three decades of the century men seemed to need to get together in social groups. The temper of the times has been expressed by Foster Rhea Dulles in *The United States Since 1865:*

> There was a phenomenal increase in fraternal orders. Masons, Oddfellows, Knights of Pythias, and Elks were joined by Shriners, Good Templars, Druids, and Gophers in such profusion that the land seemed to be covered with temples, camps, clans, castles, and conclaves. The United States proved itself to be a "nation of joiners." The conventions and balls, picnics and sociables of the myriads of new clubs and societies were an enlivening addition to the traditional church suppers.

Baseball, Burlesque, and Buffalo Bill added to the social stew already well seasoned by the advent of Jazz. It was an exciting time filled with music and mummery. This period, too, saw the great revival of the pageant impulse. It was as if the nation had shucked off its old coat of tragedy and assumed the motley in an effort to forget a century of war and social turmoil. Withington, in his *English Pageantry—an Historical Outline*, writing of this general era and the following years in the United States, said:

> Hardly a day goes by that one does not see in the daily papers accounts of a pageant just given or about to be given. The whole country is in a fair way to become pageant mad; and in this madness pageantry has taken on many different shapes.

35

One of those shapes developed in St. Louis where we see the origin of the Veiled Prophet balls and procession. The first such pageant, held in the autumn of 1878, featured seventeen floats: 1. The Glacial Period of Winter; 2. The Chariot of the Sun; 3. Primitive Animals; 4. Fiends of Darkness; 5. The Centaur; 6. Flora; 7. Proserpine and Pluto; 8. Golden Globe; 9. Demeter; 10. Triptolemus; 11. Plowing; 12. Fruits; 13. Bacchus; 14. Industry; 15. Wealth; 16. "The Veiled Prophet"; 17. Silenus.

In New Orleans the Mardi Gras took a new lease on life and began to get more and more spectacular toward the end of the century.

It was during this period as well that the Philadelphia Mummers Parade as now constituted got its start. The *Public Ledger* for January 3, 1876, carried many things on its front page: the dedication of Fiske University; a notice that Bishop Dupanloup had gone to Paris to urge canonization of Joan of Arc; and, as a final note, a telegram from Sioux City telling of the imminence of attack from four hundred Sioux Indians. There was a notice that a man was injured in a tavern brawl, that a sailor had been hit on the head by a barrel, that a child had been hurt at play; nowhere on the front page was the Mummers Parade mentioned. Over on the editorial page, however, was carried the following notice:

> When it was all over, when 1875 had ceased to be and 1876 had been saluted with the old salutation, "Farewell to the old year, all hail to the new," there was a revulsion of feeling such as made the ordinary celebrations of the birth of a new year a happy relief. The bands of fantastically dressed men and boys much more numerous and gaily dressed than usual, had an appreciative audience before whom to parade. At midnight, they had been completely forgotten but when the grand outburst of popular feeling had subsided, the one step from the sublime to the ridiculous was quickly taken, and the "carnival" of fun and exuberance began. Such processions as were organized during the rest of the night and on Saturday were never seen before on so broad a scale in "the Quaker City." Their frolics are not to be lightly censured, but it would perhaps be well if, like the grand expression of public sentiment which was the great feature of the celebration, they become Century plants, blooming but once in a hundred years.

All comment, however, was not as caustic as the above, for in that same paper, under the heading "Local Affairs," the following notice was printed:

On New Year's day the weather was as uncomfortable as usual lately, but it seemed to have little or no effect on the spirits of our citizens, who crowded the streets and made the city very lively during the entire day and evening. There was probably a larger display of bunting and flags than was ever before seen in Philadelphia, in the business portions of the city, the unornamented buildings being the exception and not the rule. At many establishments the displays were marked by great good taste and artistic beauty.

The Fantasticals or "Shooters" were out in force during the whole day, and caused much boisterous amusement. Indians and squaws, princes and princesses, clowns, columbines and harlequins, negroes of the minstrel-hall type, Chinese and burlesque Dutchmen, bears, apes, and other animals promenaded the streets to the music of calethumpian, cow-bells, or the more dignified brass bands, and kept up their racket until late at night. Independence Hall was the grand objective point for them all, and the old building received many a cheer, both burlesque and serious. In the middle of the day several of these parties united in one grand parade and made a striking display.

The contrast to the Veiled Prophet Procession of approximately the same period is striking. In St. Louis the floats predominated, and were stately and serene; in Philadelphia, the paraders predominated and were obviously far from stately and serene.

Some idea of the early Philadelphia celebrations can be had from an article in *Scribner's Monthly*, July 1881:

He explains that the accordion is not what it was; he broke it last New Year's Night "out bell-snicklin." This custom is known in other parts of the Neck as "New Year's Shooting." On New Year's Eve, crowds of men and boys dress themselves in fantastic costumes and roam through the Neck and lower part of the city all night. This custom, doubtless a remnant of the Old English Christmas "mumming," grows year by year in Philadelphia, and the mummers, becoming bolder, penetrate as far north as Chestnut Street.

37

This is the earliest mention of the custom known as mumming, and may be the beginning of the association of the word "mummer" with the Parade.

In the late 1880s many Fancy Clubs sprung up in South
Philadelphia, these included the William Banner; George A. Baird;
Independents; Thomas Clements, Sr.; and Thomas Clements, Jr.
This seems to have been the period when the clubs were named
after local celebrities. The Thomas Clements, Sr., Club paraded on
New Year's Day, 1888, on South Broad Street, and without
competition was awarded $25.00, the first cash prize in Mummers'
and Shooters' history.

Many of the early clubs, especially the Comics, had amusing
names: the Early Risers, Dark Lanterns, Hardly Ables, White
Caps, Energetic Hoboes, Red Onions, Corinthians, Half and Half,
Cucumbers, and White Turnips. There seems to have been a lack of
historical appreciation in the early Mummers except for two clubs
named the Penn Treaty and the Washington.

These clubs early established the pattern they were to follow
through the years. They were purely local in nature; that is, each
group represented some particular section of Philadelphia. At first
these groups did not feel the need to organize further; they were
satisfied with individual parades. This attitude changed when local
merchants began contributing cash prizes, together with various
types of merchandise, for the best group.

Before this, many organization vied with each other to attract
the Mummers to their places of business. Saloons would put out
huge spreads to entice the paraders: great roasts of venison,
turkey, chicken, and hams, ale and beer were all on the menu—
free. This sometimes held up the parades for hours, which is
perhaps why the custom is no longer practiced. Those of us who
decry the departure of the free-lunch-counter from our favorite
saloons must sympathize with the Mummer of today. Think of
what he is missing.

Many stores, especially bakers, would donate cakes to the best
marchers. Quite often ladies of the neighborhood baked cakes for
their favorite groups. One sedate lady of today remembers that as
a child she waited expectantly for the Mummers to show up,
hoping that they would forget her house so that she could have
the cake to herself. She reports that they never failed to show up.

The Mummers would be accompanied by a wagon known as a
"cake-wagon," used to gather up donations. Later, usually within
a few days, cake-cutting parties would be held, at which time the

prize cakes would be cut and served. This was always an excuse for another party, providing the participants had sufficiently recovered from the New Year's parties.

From these cake-cutting parties sprung annual New Years' fund-raising balls, which became the social highlights of the year. The Silver Crown Club held its annual ball at the Musical Fund Hall for many years. Other clubs in the city followed suit in other large halls. These balls were organized by the clubs to entertain their friends as well as to raise funds for their costumes.

Rivalry was high in these parades, and tempers were not always smooth; below is the recollection of an early parade by Mr. Harry Hodgson:

> In all these years, while intense rivalry existed between the clubs and sectional feeling was strong, no serious clashes ever occurred, although the cup that cheers frequently "cheered too loudly" for some of the marchers, with one unfortunate exception when two clubs came together in a nasty battle in the vicinity of Second and Federal streets, as a result of which one of the clubs never marched again and the other after a few years' existence disappeared from the scene. The writer of this article witnessed a small part of this fray as a very small boy, two things remaining vivid in his recollections; one, of a man dressed as a clown with one foot through the head of a bass drum and using his other foot to finish the job; and the other, that of my father who had taken me to see the paraders, gathering me under his arm like a bundle and making a hasty getaway from the musketry which started to take place.

It was often the custom for the winning clubs to visit rival clubs and serenade them with the "Funeral March." This would be the signal for the losers to dash forth; and the fight would be on. One such fight, between the Baseler Club and the Clements, Sr., Club, resulted in a riot call.

Each of these early clubs had four or five officers: a captain, two lieutenants, a music director, and a speech director. John C. Dougherty, as captain of the Washington New Year's club, received the first New Year's permit ever issued. It was issued on December 15, 1887, by John Lamon, the Superintendent of Police.

39

A leader or speech director was named by the paraders. This leader had a special little dance step, and recited a speech, usually in rhyme. Here is one preserved by C. B. Tustin, Sr., an old-time Mummer, who dated it in 1930 as "of about 50 years ago or more."

NEW YEAR'S SPEECH

Mr. and Mrs. _____ I wish you a Merry Christmas and a Happy New Year, a pocket full of money and cellar full of Beer. You Sons, Daughters, Men, Maids, and all who dwell within your walls I say we do not come for what you give us, merely your hearts to cheer, set your whiskey on the table and we will drink while we are able otherwise set it on the shelf and we will go and help ourself.

We have traveled this neighborhood around and around and many good Neighbors we have found. We have Clowns, Indians, and Niggers and Guns and Pistols with one and two sets of triggers.

Now I am going to tell you about Old Clarkey who saves up his Fips and goes to the Horse Market buying up all the three legged Rips, them that look like Ghosts he puts in the ground for fence posts and them that look like snails he puts in the post for fence rails, also Old Man Simon sets back of the stove roasting his shins looking at the Greenbacks come rolling in, now I will turn my speech another way and nothing more about Clarkey or Old Man Simon I will have to say.

Now there's Old Man Irvin puts in Pumps old and new and goes up and down the road dancing Hopty Doodle Doo. Now there's Charley B_____ thinks himself a sporter because he courts Jacob Y_____ daughter, he looks so flip he swallowed his Mother's scrubing brush and the bristles grew out of his upper lip.

Now give us Whiskey, give us Gin and with sweet music we will begin, music sweet, music loud, we are the happiest New Years Shooters who travel the road. Now there's Old Man Hess thinks himself a boss because he drives a little black Hoss.

Now the crimson sun sets streaming far down the distant West the ones we loved so dearly have gone to their Heavenly Rest. Now I hope your Horses and Cows will all grow large and your Hogs turn into lard. Now we have traveled where no man dare but the Wild Cat, Tiger, and the Bear.

Room! Room! my brave and gallant boys and girls give us room to rhyme and we will show you our slightest activities upon a New Years time. We also have taken the liberty to come here to remember you from year to year. God has spared us one year more that we may come into your door. We will eat and drink with all good cheer that we may live another year. Now I will conclude my speech as I have nothing more to say so get back boys and fire away.

(Band plays and march in house, get refreshments, dance for about a half-hour or until another company comes then a fight or get out.)

We can notice some similarity between the verse remembered by Mr. William F. Field which goes:

> Here I stand before your door
> As we stood the year before.
> Set your bottles on the shelves,
> We have whiskey enough to help ourselves.

and the first paragraph of Mr. Tustin's speech. This is the only complete speech of the early Mummers which has been located, and approximately dated at the early post-Civil War period. As we read it we can sense some of the elements. We can assume it was used for a specific group from the use of personal names and situations. It was light in nature, and not always complimentary; its purpose seemed to be to razz as much as anything else; however, this was not always so. Here is a fragment of a speech by Captain Jacob S. Herbert, Sr., of the B. E. Stevens Club given on New Year's Day 1895:

Mr. & Mrs. & Mostly friends so kind
   We turn out today to try & brighten up your mind
And to make your hearts feel both light and gay
   And to enjoy yourselves on this New Years Day
Now as New Years day comes but once a year
   We celebrate it with frolic fun and good cheer
And may we be thankful to the Lord
   For he gives to us the best he can afford
Our desire is to please you and do it is our aim
   And bring no disgrace on any one's name

41

To you we are known may our pleasure be great
　　That today with our friends once more we can meet
Because we turn out as shooters and not as dubs
　　And pay you our honor as the B. E. Stevens Club
Now my band will give a screech
　　Of music Loud and Music Sweet
O how sweet that music does sound
　　For it gladdens the hearts of all around
And as our echo dies away
　　A short tune for you my band will play.

Again we have some fleeting clichés from Tustin's speech —"music sweet, music loud"—but the tone is quite different, and the material itself seems closer to Mr. J. S. Herbert, Jr.'s own contribution (he presented this in a letter in 1930) than to the folk clichés. Mr. Tustin's appears closer to the folk clichés of the Mummers' Play than do those of Mr. Herbert.

The following speech has much more the flavor of having been handed down from one generation to another. Despite its dating to 1931, it has reference to Teddy Roosevelt big-game hunting, Cook and Peary discovering the North Pole, and George Washington. Here are the greetings by J. W. M. of the Lobster Club:

Mr. and Mrs. _____ We wish you a Merry Christmas & Happy New Year,
　　the old one is gone and the new one is here,
This is the day we love so dear
　　and to every household brings good Cheer.

The year just passed we had hard times to endure,
　　May 1931 bring Prosperity to the poor.

Cook and Peary went to find the North Pole.
When they got there, they found it very cold;
But what they discovered, we never found out
So they will have to try again and take another route.

Roosevelt went to Africa to shoot Teddy Bears,
And to drive away dull sorrow and cares.
Through the wilds of Africa, he did roam
But he was glad to get back to Home Sweet Home.

Now we have had men of the greatest Fame,
George Washington is one I'm going to name;
He fought for his Country was brave and true,
And he upheld our Flag, the Red, White and Blue.

Now please kind friends, just bear in mind,
A faithful friend is hard to find;
And when you find one that is True
Don't give up the old one for the New.

Now my friends with your kind attention
Some of the Lobster boys I'm going to mention;
There's our Captain, he is as good as gold;
He made his own suit so I've been told.

They say he just finished it the other night,
Just look it over, it's sure Out of Sight,
John Fintcher he thought himself fly,
When he paid 1.50 for a plush necktie,
Of the bargain he thought he got the best;
When he paid 8 bucks for a low-cut vest.
Now there's Theo Hazzard, the talk of the Town,
That boy's known for miles around;
He stopped a drinking, just for fun,
And half the breweries are on the bum.
Now we are going to have the Energetic Band,
It is one of the finest in the Land;
The music they play so loud and sweet,
You just bet your life it can't be beat.

Now with this my speech comes to a close,
As my boys outside, they sure are froze;
If you ain't got whiskey, beer or gin,
Just open your doors and let us in,
Then you'll see how good you'll feel
When our Band strikes up the Bummers Reel.

HERE
WE STAND
BEFORE
YOUR DOOR

The above has been reproduced exactly as written. Here we
have the general pattern of the Tustin speech: greetings to the
householders; joshing references to the people present; the call for
"whiskey and gin"; entrance of players; entertainment of sorts; 43
and finally the exit. Although J. W. M.'s (probably John Wesley

Myers) speech has reference to 1931, obvious elements of the past are present: the call for whiskey and gin, the reference to music both loud and sweet. This is probably the last complete speech of the Mummers, as no others have come to light. The only other materials available are some fragments, a popular one of the Mummers of the past was this one:

> Here we stand before your door
> As we stood the year before
> Give us whiskey, give us gin
> Open the door and let us in.

For a tamer version, the Mummers had this recitation:

> Here we stand before your door
> As we stood the year before;
> Give us coffee nice and hot,
> And we'll make this a happy spot.

Some of the flavor of the past was caught by Joe Ferko, a longtime Mummer, in the following reminiscence:

"When I was in South Philadelphia with the old Fralinger String Band, those days people used to give the various clubs cakes. We would go to our various friends, knock at the door, and then we would open the door a little and say:

> "Here we stand before your door
> Just as we did the year before.
> Give us whiskey, give us gin
> Open the door and let us in."

"The band would start to play a number and we would go in and come out with the cake, and about two weeks after New Year's we would have a so-called cake cutting. Anyone who presented us with a cake would receive two free tickets and then we would go and have a so-called cake cutting."

44

The various Mummer bands would be followed by a horse-drawn cart where the gift cakes would be deposited; this custom and the one above described by Joe Ferko was practiced in the early years of this century, but the custom was obviously based on an older one.

A clue to another practice of early Mummers may be found in this variant of their presentation speech:

> Here we stand at your front door
> Just as we did the year before.
> Open the door and let us in,
> Give us all a drink of gin.
> Or better give us something hot,
> A steaming bowl of Pepper Pot.

Many of the families in the "Neck," that portion of South Philadelphia from which the early Mummers came, would serve the famous local soup, pepper pot, to the visitors. The women would make the soup days in advance so that they, too, would have some time for celebrating over the year's end. Great pots, more stew than soup in some cases, would simmer on the wood-burning stoves waiting for the cold and hungry marchers from Smoky Hollow, Stone-House Lane, Prospect Bank, Martin's Village, Greenwich Point, Peacock Farms, and Gardner's Crossing to claim their share. The recipe for pepper pot varies as do many of the customs of the Mummers, an independent lot. An old Philadelphia family recipe dating back 150 years will be found in the Appendix.

The real start of the Philadelphia Mummers Parade as we know it was during the nineteenth century. At the beginning of the century, the Parade fell under the ban of the law, and remained so for the next fifty years. It was a lusty baby, however, and its growth could not be stunted. Other organizations continued the custom of parading, and soon the police looked the other way.

The great period of growth which saw many clubs organized began after the Civil War. Among the earliest clubs were: the Bright Star, the Morning Star, the Golden Crown, and the Silver Crown. The greatest expansion took place after 1875.

The Thomas Clements, Sr., Club was awarded the first cash prize in Mummers' history, $25.00 in 1888. This marked the beginning of the organized parades. Rivalry was still strong, but the groups got together into more organized parades, and mer-

45

chants put up prizes for the best marchers. The route of the Mummers was along Market Street, and there was no set order or time, the clubs marched at any time between 9 A.M. and 5 P.M.

By the end of the nineteenth century, the Philadelphia Mummers Parade was a well-established tradition, and was growing rapidly. So much a part of the community had it become, that H. Bart McHugh, a newspaperman at the time, decided to have the Mummers help Philadelphia greet the new century. Taking his idea to J. Hampton Moore, secretary to Mayor Ashbridge, he outlined it. There would be an official city reception for the paraders on New Year's Eve at City Hall; the Hall itself would be lighted with thousands of electric lights, and there would be fireworks. Then on New Year's Day there would be an official parade sponsored by the city and prizes awarded, appropriated by the city. Mayor Ashbridge agreed, and the City Council put up $5,000 in prizes. At first the Mummers refused to go along with the idea—individuals to the last, they resented city interference with their Parade. Finally, after many meetings and much talk, they agreed to help the city greet the new century, and the show was on.

KINGS FOR A DAY

The twentieth century dawned clear and cold, and a strong wind swept up Broad Street from the north to greet the Mummers. Spectators had to bundle up and stamp their feet to keep warm. The marchers were in a merry mood and kept up a rapid pace. The official history of the Mummers Parade dates from this, the first city-sponsored Parade. It was small by current standards, as only 2,500 men participated in the four Fancy Clubs and eight Comic Clubs in the Parade. John H. Baizley rode at the head of the line astride a white horse; even today old Shooters remember Baizley and his horse as part of the tradition of the Parade in the early part of the century.

To the Silver Crown Club, oldest in line, went the honor of leading the Fancy Clubs "up the Street." John Hoar captained the Silver Crown Club, and received great rounds of applause as, garbed in an elaborate cape supported by a line of page boys, he strutted up the wind-swept street. The Elkton Association followed: its Shooters, covering a half mile, received great rounds of applause throughout the entire route of the Parade. The George A. Furnival Association was third in line; the John F. Slater Club brought up the rear.

The Katzenjammer Band led off the Comic Clubs, and were enthusiastically joined by the White Caps, Dark Lanterns, Hardly Old Timers, Energetic Hoboes, Mixed Pickles, the Daniel Duane Club, and the Ivy Leaf. The Comic section was the larger and the members seemed to enjoy themselves more since they were not impeded by the heavy wind as were the Fancy Club marchers.

One of the local newpapers carried the following item:

> The City knew them a century ago. Ragamuffins they were about that time, and ragamuffins the half of them looked yesterday.

47

But the City had called them together with an offer of money prizes, and thus Philadelphia saw on the first day of the twentieth century a procession that Momus himself could not have devised.

Mayor Ashbridge and his cabinet sat in the reviewing stands on the North Plaza of City Hall, together with the judges of the Parade, Barclay Warburton, Harrington Fitzgerald, and William Simpson. According to another local paper:

> . . .One coy dame in widow's weeds perked and smirked at the city's rulers, and finally like a country hoyden, almost dragged the Mayor from the stands.

For this first Parade, Broad Street was roped off from Reed Street to Girard Avenue. After the march was completed, the men went north to Kensington where other prizes awaited them.

The trip up Broad Street was marked by great joviality and was well received by the crowds that lined the street. The Comics created much amusement by poking fun at the horseless carriage.

The prizewinners of the first Parade were:

FANCY DIVISION

First Prize	$300.00	Elkton Association
Second Prize	250.00	Furnival Association
Third Prize	150.00	Silver Crown Club
Fourth Prize	100.00	John F. Slater Club

COMIC DIVISION

First Prize	$300.00	White Caps
Second Prize	250.00	Daniel Duane Club
Third Prize	150.00	Mixed Pickles
Fourth Prize	100.00	Dark Lanterns
Fifth Prize	75.00	Katzenjammer Band
Sixth Prize	50.00	Energetic Hoboes

The other two clubs participating were awarded $25.00 each for their efforts and as an inducement to try again.

That year East Girard Avenue Business Men's Association also awarded prizes. There was an interesting difference of opinion between the two groups in picking the winners of first prize. The Girard Avenue selections were:

FANCY DIVISION

First Prize	$ 75.00	John F. Slater Club
Second Prize	50.00	Elkton Association
Third Prize	25.00	Furnival Association

COMIC DIVISION

First Prize	$ 75.00	Daniel Duane Club
Second Prize	50.00	Mixed Pickles
Third Prize	25.00	Ivy Leaf

Since that first Parade up Broad Street, the Mummers' clubs have grown in numbers and complexity. In the early days the men were all drawn from South Philadelphia; soon they began to come from all sections of the city, and some were even drawn from neighboring towns and counties. With this increase in size, competition became stronger, and the Parade more elaborate. To understand how elaborate, and how sumptuous our "ragamuffins" became, one need only look through the newspapers of the day, and discuss the Parade with old Mummers. One of the truly great Parades of all-time Mummer antics was that which greeted the year of the Great Depression.

A fine drizzle mixed with confetti greeted the Philadelphia Mummers Parade on January 5, 1929. Broad Street was a shimmering spectacle as monarchs, clowns, Indians, and devils cavorted in the mist. As the marchers moved on City Hall, great showers of confetti thrown at them from office buildings made them look as if they had come through a snow storm.

Rain had already postponed the Parade once. The Mummers were determined to strut come what may: and strut they did. Captains and clowns, devils and dancers, kings and queens blended their colors into a mighty spectrum that glowed in the mist with an eerie quality.

The drizzling rain failed to dim the enthusiasm of the record crowd gathered to watch the traditional salute and celebration of the New Year's Shooters of Philadelphia. Sidewalks and street crossings were jammed with people, many of whom had been standing for six or seven hours in order to ensure good spots from which to watch. Children sat on their parents' shoulders, old people, wrapped in blankets, sat on the curbs, peach baskets provided extra height for some and gave protection from the rain

49

for others. Shoulder to shoulder, elbow to elbow, the vast crowd waited for the first sight of the Parade.

H. Bart McHugh, the Parade's Director, had given the signal to start at Broad and Porter streets. Then, riding a white horse, he led the way followed by a retinue of twenty-five mounted police headed by Captain W. Buehler. The automobile carrying the officials of the Parade followed. After these earthly dignitaries, came the Mummer Monarchs.

The Silver Crown Club, oldest of the clubs, and again first in line, was led by Uncle Sam carrying an American flag. He wore a glistening satin robe with a magnificent train stretching behind him almost a city block. Next, marched Captain Frank Daily with a train decorated with gold, red, and purple in six sections, interwoven with ribbons of roses. The cape was supported by 120 pages in colorful robes that complemented the "King's" costume.

In the Funston Club, Captain David Crawford's spectacular costume of orange, red, and white brought great bursts of applause from the crowd. His satin train was 210 feet long, and decorated in such a way as to give the effect of a great garden. Over the head of this royal parader was a canopy of satin trimmed with white maribou and sprinkled with glittering gems and roses of red satin.

Following the gala royalty, came a galaxy of "girls," the last of the Fancies, strutting and flaunting their ersatz charms before the crowd.

The picture changed then, as the Comic Clubs took over with their broad travesties and earthy "interpretations" of local, national, and international affairs. The famous League Island Club, from the heart of the "Neck," traditional home of the Mummers, imitated the Prince of Wales hunting for big game. The shoulders of the prince were hung with lions, and he bravely clutched smaller, but no less ferocious animals in his hands. He was surrounded by cotton pickers in blackface, flappers, and clowns. "Hoover's Farmer Relief" was parodied; bootlegging was carried on in the City Hall Annex; Chicago bandits robbed banks. Boo Boo Hoof, a local racketeer, was presented as "Bo Bo Hoof," and immediately began presenting "gifts" to blindfolded policemen. Nearby, attired as an Eskimo, walked "Miss South Pole," who announced herself as "Commander Byrd's latest lady friend." Later that night "Miss South Pole" revealed herself as Miss Laura

Lee, a reporter, and the first to publicly flaunt the taboo of "no women allowed."

As the last of the clowns danced off, the strains of banjo and guitar, violin and clarinet, and a gorgeous shimmering of satin and silk announced the advent of the String Bands led by the Hegeman Club with scarlet-clad, mounted Heralds presenting the "Three Musketeers" in all their glory. Captain Harry Whitman led the band in a cavalier costume of white and gold. A hundred musicians followed him, all wearing soft black boots, loose trousers, gallant capes, and rolled plumed hats. Their various colors of red, white, green, black, and gold made an appropriate opening for the String Band section.

The Trixie Band was next, parading as "Musical Cossacks," and led by Edward Thompson mounted on a coal-black steed. Thomas W. Belke, captain of the band, led them in a Cossack costume of red velvet trimmed with pearls and rhinestones and gold braid. His seventy-five musicians also carried out his motif.

Then followed the Woodland String Band dressed as soldiers of the "Great War," dressed in black and white uniforms topped with shining helmets; they brought to the crowd "Memories of France."

The Octavius V. Cato Club came next, announcing themselves as "Troubadors of 1929." Their costumes of red and gold velvet trimmed with sequins appeared to be engulfed in a red mist. Their music caught the crowd's attention, and they were warmly applauded. Unknown to audience and paraders, this was to be the Cato Club's last parade, and the virtual end of Negro participation in the Philadelphia Mummers Parade.

Peter the Great, colorfully presented by the Wildwood String Band, came next, led by four mounted Heralds. Six beautifully costumed attendants preceded the throne on which sat the Czar of Old Russia. A band of seventy musicians followed, with four drummers beating out the roll of the revolution. All were dressed in gold blouses, red velvet trousers, and gold hats adorned with clusters of garnets and topped off with great plumes.

The Russians were followed by the Joseph A. Ferko String Band; with its theme of "The Moon and Stars," it drew great rounds of applause. Sky-blue satin costumes topped off with star-shaped hats of the same color formed the basis of its costume.

A magnificent collar of five points was attached to a great cape decorated with a silvery moon surrounded by smaller quarter and half moons. The jacket and trousers of the individual members were of six different colors, a different color to each column of men. The effect was of a great waving rainbow, bringing up the end of the Parade.

At Broad Street and Girard Avenue, the paraders marched east to Second Street, and "officially" disbanded. A different parade then began—the march down Second Street. By now it was almost dark and the watchers had to strain to see the Mummers through the mist. Over the shuffling of feet could be heard the clear, bell-like tones of the glockenspiel, leading the String Bands in the *Golden Slipper*. The Comic Clubs took up the tune, and did their traditional strut, waving their umbrellas to the rhythm of the dance. The spectators joined in, and old and young swept down the street.

The residents of Second Street, in South Philadelphia, known as "two-streeters," had long supplied the core of the Mummers, and now they were home. The marchers were tired but exhilarated; they were among their own and acted accordingly. The bottle was now passed openly. The entire neighborhood was out in force. The Mummers were "free," and they swung from one side of the street to the other, exuberantly greeting their friends and families. In the official Parade, the kissing of pretty girls was discouraged; here it was enthusiastically endorsed. By midnight the last Mummer had reached his limit, and the Parade was over for another year.

This 1929 Parade was a highlight in Mummer history, and the high-water mark of its greatness. Hard times were to come and go before the Parade would achieve its greatness again; but this Parade would remain in the minds of its marchers as one of the great ones.

And so it goes, each year in Philadelphia the Mummers throw out all the laws of economics; the "Kings for a Day" strut forth in pomp and glory that would send a Maharajah home to pawn his jewels. There are no limits on expenditures, the only object is to have the best costume on the "Street." These are not wealthy men, yet for this "Day of Days" they expend money with great prodigality. One day each year they play their part in satisfying man's desire to "dress up" and be someone else.

Months are spent planning the various floats and costumes to be used on New Year's Day. No Mummer wants to repeat last years' creations and, as a matter of fact, is not permitted to do so by the rules governing the Parade, and so must spend much time and money for something original. All members of the clubs and their families are employed in this effort to be the best in the show. As some of the Mummers have been marching for fifty years, the effort to avoid repetition is not always easy.

The Captain's Cape is the topic of greatest interest in the Fancy Clubs. These capes had grown from humble one-man affairs to huge trains supported by as many as 130 page boys; in fact, they grew so large that the Parade leaders felt it necessary to restrict to ten the number of page boys permitted for each cape. Even with these restrictions, a great deal of money is required by the Mummers of the Fancy Clubs; this goes for the String Bands and the Comic Clubs as well. Where does it come from?

The cost of running the clubs is shared by all members. Each member, in the old days, paid for his own costume. Men would bid in the clubs for the privilege of wearing certain costumes. This bidding was always very important, and was usually settled not by money, but by service in the organization and the good of the club. There are some stories that the prestige of a strong fist won out on occasion, but these instances were rare. The fee to appear as a certain character was usually $3.00; no other member of the club would then encroach upon this characterization. This was one rule which was invariably held to.

In the current organizational set up of the Mummers, individual groups contribute to the cost of the costumes of their members. Even with the club contributions, the Mummer is always in the hole, even if he wins first prize. An example of this may be seen in the case of David W. Crawford of the Funston Club. Crawford, one of the all-time greats, won the first prize for the best Captain in the parade in 1929. The money value of the prize was $600.00. Here are Mr. Crawford's expenses for that costume:

Satin and Labor	$1,732.00
Head-dress	250.00
Page Boys	250.00
Assistants	275.00
Carpenter	25.00
Socks	18.00
Total	$2,2550.00

To pay the expenses listed above, the Funston Club contributed $750.00; this sum added to the prize money, $600.00, still left a deficit of $1,200.00 to be met by Mr. Crawford, who won first prize! What of the many other Captains participating that day who were not fortunate enough to win?

Back in 1904, Thomas Duffy paraded as Captain of the Thomas Clements, Sr., Club. Duffy is still remembered among the Shooters as the "guy who walked with a year's pay on his back." This is not an uncommon practice with Mummers, especially the old-timers.

As the Parade is a family affair, many men have more than one costume to pay for. How do they meet the cost of their "one day in the sun"? There are many ways, all of which combine with doing-without to add to the Mummers' larder for New Year's Day. Most of these men live on a very close budget in order to spend their money on costumes. Many borrow the money, and pay it back during the year; many do without new clothes of a more conventional nature, in order to parade up Broad Street on New Year's Day in a brand new Mummers' costume. However much money the Mummer spends on his own costume, he does not neglect his family. The Shooters' families are a healthy, happy group always busy, and always looking forward to "next year."

The clubs finance themselves by running dances during the year and by the proceeds derived from operating their clubhouses. Due to the great popularity of the Parade, the various Mummers' organizations are constantly being invited to perform out of season. Most of these invitations go to the String Bands as they are of most general interest and less bulky to transport. The Comic Clubs and Fancy Club Divisions, therefore, seldom can take advantage of this chance to earn extra money. Individual String Bands have performed for such events as tobacco festivals, state fairs, the Miss America Pageant and in the Thanksgiving Day parade held by Macy's Department Store in New York City. The money earned from these appearances generally goes into the Club's treasury.

In 1947, for instance, the Joseph A. Ferko String Band received $500.00 for appearing in the Thanksgiving Day parade in New York. This sum was placed in the club's treasury, and divided equally among the members; each man was given credit on the organization's books for his share.

With the Ferko Band, receipts for the entire year are kept in the club's treasury; at the year's end, when the time comes for new costumes, the club pays half, and the individual member pays half out of his credit on the books. If the Mummer has more money to his credit than is required, he is refunded this surplus; if he is short on his half he must make up the difference.

In 1949 the American Federation of Musicians banned the cutting of new records by its members. This action caused the radio stations to look for nonunion musical groups, and their eyes fell upon the Mummers. The Bands caught on, and for a brief period almost monopolized the airwaves.

The Hegeman String Band alone sold over 100,000 recordings of "I'm Looking Over a Four-Leaf Clover"; the Joseph A. Ferko String Band received $4,000 for records it cut. Popularity, however, did not remain at this high peak after Mr. Petrillo lifted the ban on union recordings. While it lasted, the added sums of money aided the various clubs to defray expenses, and the Mummers Parade was popularized.

An additional source of income was opened up in television for at least one Mummers' Club, the Quaker City String Band. This organization played for a number of years in the early fifties over WCAU-TV on a circus program called "Big Top."

When S. Davis Wilson was mayor, he instituted a milk fund for underprivileged children, and as an aid in raising money asked the Mummers to parade for a silver cup. This first show, held in Convention Hall, was moderately successful. The tickets sold for fifty cents, but the Mummers had a hard time selling them. This parade has grown into a mammoth affair held every February in Convention Hall. Now called the "Show of Shows," it draws people from all over the eastern part of the state, invariably playing to full houses. This, too, adds to the coffers of the participating organizations.

Since that first officially sponsored march, the Mummers Parade has been constantly growing. From unwelcome ragamuffins we have seen them become "Kings for a Day," spreading their influence into all phases of the city's life. To cope with this expansion there was incorporated in 1932 the Philadelphia Mummers Association. This organization later became the Philadelphia New Year Shooters and Mummers' Association, Inc. All rules and regulations for the Parade are formed jointly by this organization and the city. A rule that no president could succeed himself was in effect from 1941 to 1958.

There has been a constant development in the strength of the Philadelphia Mummers Parade. From a humble 2,500, their number has grown to more than 15,000; and they are still growing. With the advent of television, additional sources of income have opened up for them, thus enabling greater outlay on their part. The result has been to change the Mummer from a local phenomenon to a national one. People from all over the United States are aware of his activities.

This change in the character of the Mummers Parade has given the individual marcher a new responsibility, and he is living up to it. With the growth of the Parade, comes the possibility that it will get out of the hands of the people who participate, and into the hands of commercial sponsors as has happened to some extent to the Mardi Gras and the Pasadena Rose Parade. The Mummers are strongly individualistic, however, and are not likely to put their fate into outside hands. The Parade belongs to the people and current indications are that it will remain so.

The Comic Clubs AND QUIETLY GO MAD

The earliest of all the Mummer clubs anyone can remember is the Chain Gang, which was believed to have been organized about 1846. A Comic Club as we know it today, this group organized and took a name with the expressed purpose of parading over New Year's Eve and the next day. Nothing else is known of this, the first organized club.

Shortly after the organization of the Chain Gang, some members of the Shiffler Hose Company, also known as Santa Anna's Cavalry, made the rounds in South Philadelphia on New Year's Eve and New Year's Day in costumes. They wore simple costumes and uncomplicated makeup.

In the years immediately preceding the Civil War, the residents of southeastern Philadelphia paraded on New Year's Eve and New Year's Day on a fairly regular basis. This era has become known as the lampblack period, because the marchers used a combination of lard and lampblack to disguise themselves. Wearing this disguise and, generally, with jackets turned inside out or in women's clothes, they would roam the area of Smoky Hollow, Stone-House Lane, Prospect Bank, Martin's Village, and other sections east of League Island, in southeastern Philadelphia. The paraders quite often carried stockings filled with flour with which they would "sock" unwary pedestrians.

These neighborhood excursions were discontinued for five years during the Civil War. At the war's end, many clubs were organized. Among them were the Bright Star, Morning Star, Golden Crown, and Silver Crown. Some of these clubs were short lived. For instance, by 1882-83 the Morning Star had already disbanded. These clubs were all what we would now call Fancy, though they

57

were not yet so classified, and we will look at their histories in the next chapter.

One of the first Comic Clubs organized was the Cold Water, which first paraded in 1884. This club had a notable reputation for many years, and won many prizes. In 1900 it changed its name to Forty Sevens, and continued to make the folks on the sidelines laugh. This club disbanded soon after the turn of the century, and its members joined other clubs. Many of these old Comic Clubs had picturesque names; there were: the Hardly Ables, Dill Pickles, Red Onions, Dark Lanterns, Mixed Pickles, Energetic Hoboes, and the Blue Ribbons. Later the clubs were named after prominent Philadelphians.

It is difficult to separate Comic from Fancy Clubs in these early days for some clubs started as Comic and ended Fancy. A good example is the Lobster Club. Following is an anonymous history of the club, written in 1930. The transcription is exactly as written; no attempt to edit has been made.

Lobster N.Y.A.

How Organized

On December 7, 1907 a crowd of the boys were in the saloon of Fred Ashenbock at the corner of 6th and Wolf sts, then our favorite meeting place, when in came Bill Carey who after looking us over said that we looked like a "bunch of lobsters," which was at once suggested as a good name for a Club.

And that is how it started.

Fred Ashenbock gave us the use of his stable loft as a meeting place, promised to pay for the first band, which he did, and our first Captain was Bill Carey, better known as "Reddy," this because of his indirect selection of the name.

He was Captain for two years, the Club then being comic he was made up as a Lobster.

Being cramped for rooms, we removed to John Fentcher's N.w cor of 6th & Ritner sts one square below where we started, we went from place to place in the way of old time "shooters." After moving it was decided to go "Fancy" which it is today, it has won more first prizes for Club and Captain than any other club taking part in the New Year's Parade only missing in 1919 due to the boys not coming from France in large enough numbers to take part in the parade.

The membership is composed of men in all walks of life, whose hobby is "shooting", and the Club promises the finest turn-out both in numbers and costuming, that has ever been seen in Broad street.

As the early clubs shifted from Fancy to Comic or from Comic to Fancy, so did the early Mummers. Members moved from club to club. In a letter [unedited here] written in 1930, Fred A. Winkler gives us some idea of parade perambulations:

> ...and will say that Ive been New Year Shooting for the last 30 years and still in line with them every year and am one of the Organizers of the League Island New Year Ass'n and have been and Individual prize winner nearly every year only the year going by Ive been a winner in line with League Island N.Y. Asss'nn as the funniest character as Singing in the bath-Tub. Ive been out shooting with the Silver-Crown—Furnival—Thomas Clements-Firth all Fancy Club's then I fell in line with the Comic Club's the White Caps. M.A. Bruder, Murray Biggins, League Island which 'm still a member of. . . .

As members moved freely about, the clubs themselves split into fragments, and then the fragments split, they too crossing the line from Comic to Fancy or in reverse. The Point Breeze Club was formed out of a factional split in the Silver Crown Club. The Point Breeze Club split, and part of it became the Grays Ferry Club. This too split and became the George A. Furnival Club, which later split, part of it becoming the Klein Club, and in time the William J. Funston Club.

The mobility of the individual Mummers, and the fragmentation of the clubs, makes it impossible to keep track of individual clubs and Mummers, except for the ones that stayed around for a fairly long period. Apparently the formation of a club for Shooting was as often as not spontaneous, and just as often the inspiration was arrived at in a neighborhood saloon or on a street corner. Here is J. Wesley Myers' account of the founding of the Frank A. Collins Club, a Comic Club now no longer parading:

59

> Herewith is the history of the Frank Collins Club—On Thursday evening October 13, 1922, in the rear room of the saloon of Frank Collins, then at the corner of Third and Tree sts, it was

suggested by J. Foley that a New Year Club be organized; which was right there and then begun.

The following were actively engaged in the Club's organization: J. Foley was chosen as President, George Ellis Vice President, Frank Collins whose name the Club bears was elected Treasurer, and Edgar Neass and Andy Gray were made Financial and Recording secretaries respectively. . . .

The Comic Clubs are most representative of the Parade of the past. If you were to recreate the Mummers of old, they would come closest to the Comics of today. However, the Comics have not stood still and over the years they have developed into remarkably clever performers. All individualists, their yearly offerings are always hilarious depictions of the current scene. In 1950 they poked fun at Stalin, and 1963 they likened the problems of U Thant to the situation of the old woman who lived in a shoe. In 1950 they poked fun at conditions in the Schuylkill River and helped dredge it in a clever float; and in 1963 they featured "Krooschef" and his puppet Castro. In 1967 they poked fun at Mia and Frank Sinatra, the White House wedding of Luci Johnson and Pat Nugent, and topped all off with a spoof on "Winchester Cathedral." In 1970 they hit the Hippie cheek and jowl, and married Tiny Tim and his Miss Vicki over and over again. In the year 2000, they will no doubt greet the twenty-first century as they did the twentieth—with truth and spoof, honesty and humor.

However we look at them, the Comics will reflect us, our city, and our prejudices. Our "mirror" will faithfully reflect our prejudices and follies, our fads and foibles. With this rapier or bludgeon, however, they still retain their own individuality. In their ranks will always be found the traditional figures of the Devil, the Dude, and the comic Irishman. In the past a favorite costume was the jacket, turned inside out, with cards sewn on it; now this is discouraged as being too "common." Another ancient antic now frowned upon is the carrying of sticks with dice on the ends of them; it seems that today's Mummer is not to be trusted with this possibly lethal weapon. However, their most important symbol, their golden slippers, has retained its color and significance. Once you have seen those golden slippers doing the Golden Slipper Strut you will be closer to understanding Philadelphia and its residents.

The Comic Clubs are divided into Groups and Brigades. The Group is the smaller of the two. Both units present pretty much the same material; however, the Brigades, being larger, are usually more elaborate.

The themes are usually taken from newspaper headlines, popular fads, and the comic strips. Television was a strong influence in the 1951 Parade; there were representations of "Uncle Milty," the "Old Gold Dancing Girls," and "TV's King and Queen." Charlie Chaplin and Abe Lincoln are often seen, as are Popeye and Olive Oyl. The most popular cartoon strip is Li'l Abner, and year after year his chief characters are presented; the most popular one in the 1951 Parade was Evil-eye Fleagle.

It is in their floats burlesquing current history that the Comic Clubs are at their best. A great deal of work is done on these floats, and no punches are pulled. One of the big hits of the 1951 Parade was a float by the Purul Club, called "Manor Homes—The Veteran's Dream." The "homes" consisted of one outhouse with venetian blinds. Philadelphia water has been burlesqued off and on for the past twenty years, and will probably continue to be burlesqued for the next twenty, as the Comic Clubs never give up once they get their sights set on a target.

All is not buffoonery in the Comic ranks, however. Many elaborate floats are planned and built at great expense. After the 1947 Parade, there was some criticism to the effect that the Comic Clubs were getting too fancy. This, however, does not appear to be the case. True, the floats are elaborate, but the themes are humorous. The Comic Clubs are in the business to make people laugh, and as long as they do so, there seems little reason to object to their floats being too fancy.

A three-pronged attack is launched yearly: the Comic, the Fancy, and the Musical. All three categories take on aspects of the other. However, each group has a favorite weapon. In the Comic Clubs it is satire. As Harry Potamkin has put it:

> . . .local politics received a number of brutal blows from the mummers. The character of these "set-ups" is much like the typical clown's brigade of a circus or the slapstick pantomime of Mack Sennett's Keystone cops. Indeed this comic mummery is the elementary and elemental theatre of satire, the satire that leaves no scar, and is not distant from the farcial half of the

61

Second Shepherds' Play. It is the fun-making portion of the Philadelphia Mummers' Parade that makes the affair tolerable.

The satire of the Mummers is of the bludgeon not the rapier; the Mummer instinct is for the jugular. The Mummers have always handled their satire with a heavy hand; occasionally there are breaches of good taste, but in general this is not the case. In the past the field of politics has been a favorite topic; they have lampooned city, state, and national political figures and policies. In 1948 Councilman O'Halloran forbade this practice:

> We're going to keep politics as much as possible out of this year's Parade. As long as I am Chairman, no club will start up Broad Street with any caricatures or skits ridiculing members of the National, State, or City administrations, or any persons prominent in local politics. And that goes regardless of which party the victim may belong to.

The only voice raised in protest was that of the Philadelphia *Evening Bulletin,* which said on its editorial page on December 31, 1947: "The smart cookie doesn't take a repressive attitude toward fun-poking. He realizes that a joke squelched one way is sure to blossom forth in another; and anyway, if his slip shows, he wants to know about it." The right of a people to criticize its leaders is a necessary one; when it is forbidden it places a serious handicap on the electorate, and robs its leaders of a necessary barometer of public opinion. This fact of life, however, is apparently not evident to the city fathers and to this day, Comic Clubs violating this unwritten rule seldom win prizes for their spoofs of local political ineptitude.

The Philadelphia Comic paraders agree with Keyserling that "To take things too seriously is a sign of inferiority." This attitude still carries over, even with the restrictions of today. Each of the Comic Clubs has a personality of its own. The longtime watcher gets to expect certain reactions from specific clubs. The secret is to watch over many years. The four clubs parading today in the Comic ranks have very evident individual characteristics.

The club that fought the ban on the use of blackface makeup hardest was the Hammond. This organization is strongly family dominated. It stresses the individual contribution. The clowns bunch up before they go before the judges, and then go in one wild whirling mass around City Hall. The effect is of the long-ago Saturnalia, the Roman release of tensions—the *Pausea Vitae* so necessary for the people facing the New Year. This club matches the rhythm and riotous reaction of the Florentines of old.

The Florentines celebrated, at the beginning of the Lenten season, a "Day of Misrule," when the Abbots of Unreason held sway. Its parades or processions had numerous themes—moral, mythological, historical, political, or comic. The processions featured gorgeous floats and masks designed by leading artists of their day. The famous Florentine artist, Leonardo da Vinci, is said to have contributed two masks exhibited during the carnival that followed the selection of Pope Leo X.

Ballads were written and sung in observance of these parades; each stanza closed with some such refrain as:

> We dance and sing and prance and fling,
> Tis grace that makes us glad.
> No greater bliss can be,
> Than he who piously goes mad!
> Then let us all go mad, go mad, go mad!
> Then let us all go mad!

These festivals of laughter, consecrated to the Abbots of Unreason, the King of the Bean, the Bishop of Fools, or the Lords of Misrule were common throughout Europe on feast days, a time when people relaxed, donned gay-colored costumes, and forgot the world for a day. The Hammond Club catches this spirit more than any other of the Comic Clubs in the Parade. Their choice of subject matter for mayhem is also unique. Their float in 1963 set the stage for their socially oriented presentation: "Not Red—Not Dead," and depicted the values of negotiation long before President Johnson's "Consensus." Their other important float that year reiterated their theme: "It Takes Two to Tango."

They followed this in 1964 by celebrating Joseph A. Hammond's fiftieth anniversary as a Mummer, although his career predated the founding of the club by Philip J. Hammond, Sr., on February 9, 1946.

63

Fascinated by outer space, the Hammond Club consistently comes up with floats out of this world. In 1965 it was the space camera satellite, snapping shots of a smiling moon. The float,

"The Moon Smiles on Space," was well received by a space-age audience. The following year, the audience rejoiced to a "Marriage in Space" in which the couples involved indulged in space splicing of a sort created only by superior comics.

In 1967 Hammond abandoned outer space for far-away historic representations: "Ghenghis Khan" and "Attila the Hun" were billed as "all time nice guys." In 1970 they returned to the "future" with a float urging "Building for the 1976 Centennial."

The personality of this club is portrayed in its publicity photographs, most of them showing hundreds of paraders. The Philip J. Hammond Club always depicts Mummers en masse. This characteristic is most evident as they go around City Hall before the judges. They are a dancing, joyful mob, and they roar around City Hall, giving the individual Mummer a chance to move with his brothers in a rhythmic reincarnation of their ancestors and of a great Philadelphia tradition.

Probably the largest Mummer Group in any category is the Liberty Clowns Comic Club, boasting 5,000 members. This club was organized on a snowy night in 1936. Its founder, Billy Torelli, used his father's barber shop at 1626 Ellsworth Street as a headquarters. Later the seat of command was moved to Billy's own barber shop in South Philadelphia, where he ruled until his death in 1967.

The Liberty Clowns are noted for their floats, which are often tied in with local events. They are the only Comic Club to list the individual Mummers participating in the Parade. There is a strong streak of ego in this club, inculcated no doubt by its founder. Torelli had a long history with the Mummers, moving from club to club and from Fancy to Comic, before he founded his own club. His own report is of interest. Following is an interview with him:

Q. How much preparation as far as time is concerned goes into your presentation? I mean over the years. When do you start for next year?

A. I start in August. I already have the sample badges out for next year. I'm changing the colors to red, white, and blue for the big badges—the captain's badges.

Q. How many years have you been first in line for permits?

At the turn of the century there was no competition for prizes to encourage the elaborate costuming of today. William Cryder (*left*) and George Stroby (*right*), accompanied by two unidentified Shooters, participated for many, many years.

A Fancy club costume illustrates a variation on a perennial
favorite — knights of old.

The exuberance of the Strut is one of the most appealing features of the Parade to the thousands of spectators.

This Viking shows the imaginative blend of reality and fantasy that is basic to the themes of the Fancy Clubs.

A contestant for the
"Most Handsome Costume" prize.

Make-up to complement the costume
has replaced black-face in recent years.

A String Band captain leads his Club.

A String Band forms for the judging in front of City Hall—The climax of the long march up Broad Street.

A Fancy Club getting set to go. The statue of the Quaker City's Billy Penn atop City Hall Tower in the background presides over a very "un-Quaker" affair.

It's a family affair on New Year's Day. Some Mummers start as infants and continue as long as they are able to go up the Street.

The Purul Comic Club in "Jokers Wild."

"Wheelmen" of the Hammond Comic Club.

A. I started in 1940 going up to City Hall there, at 4 o'clock on a Sunday afternoon, the office didn't open up the next morning til 9 o'clock, to get the permits, so that was about 17 hours I guess. From 1940 all the way up to 1953. The city put a stop to it, and we don't have to go for no more permits, they give us a blanket permit what they call.

Q. I thought I saw your picture.

A. I was in there every year, up to 53.

Q. What were some of the old Comic Clubs?

A. Well I paraded with the—I started in 1925 with the M. A. Bruder Club, and that was a nice big club. And I also went with the Frank Collins Club in 1927, 26 I paraded with the League Island, 28 I paraded with the George B. McClernand, 29 I paraded with League Island, 1930 I paraded in the fancy division with the Silver Crown Club, and won the first real clown prize, 150 bucks, 1931 I paraded back in the comics with the League Island, in 1932 I paraded with the George B. McClernand Club, and in 1933 was no prize money, and 10 clubs went up Broad Street, the rest went into the stadium, where they had paid admission there.

Q. Yeh I remember.

A. And I paraded with League Island on Broad Street.

Q. Joe Ferko stayed out.

A. Yeh I got the letter right in my pocket, the clubs that paraded there from the *Bulletin*, anyhow, 1934 there was no parade at all on Broad Street, it was a rainy day, not a hard rain a drizzle, and some of the clubs paraded the neighborhood, in the rain. Then in 1935, George B. McClernand became president, Parade Director, and got the Parade back to $12,000 dollars, and since that day on we been parading, and in 1936 I organized my own club, and been marching ever since.

Q. How do you feel about the rule forbidding the Mummers to use political themes?

65

A. Well the city don't want that stuff in the parade, if they do have it, both parties will be uh knocked. They just don't want it so you can't take it out.

Q. Do you know anything about the old days, the cake-wagon? Joe Ferko was telling me something about it.

A. Well I'm not as old as Joe Ferko. All I can tell you is what I heard about that.

Q. Yes?

A. Well, they just went around all the neighborhoods and the neighbors they give 'em cakes, drinks, and they would parade, you know.

Q. Did they have a saying they used?

A. Have what?

Q. A saying.

A. Whata you mean saying?

Q. Joe had something about: "Here I stand before your door."

A. Well you see he knows because like I said he's much older than I am. He paraded in them days, while I didn't; see?

The Joseph J. Purul Club was founded on April 15, 1936, by Joseph A. Purul, Sr., and participated in its first parade on January 1, 1937. It is the most dignified of the Comic Clubs, the members relying more on characterization than on comedy. This club often depends on newspaper headlines for ideas. In the 1951 Parade, it featured "Flying Saucers" and "Brinks Self Service," two items that had been very popular in the papers during 1950. Their publicity pictures for *The Mummers Magazine* make a striking contrast to those of the Hammond Club. Purul's pictures usually depict individuals or, at most, trios. Generally there was a personal note from the founder, when he was alive. A typical one was:

Dear Friends of the Mummers:
The Joseph A. Purul New Year Association
was organized April 15, 1936 as a Comic entry
in the Philadelphia Mummers Parade. It has
paraded uninterruptedly since January 1, 1937.

Each year the Purul Comics endeavor to exhibit
a bigger and better show for the citizens and
guests of the City of Brotherly Love. The
competitive spirit of the individual members

and groups makes this Comic Club almost a
mummer parade in itself.

Colorful and novel costumes, original and
unique ideas set forth this Comic Club as
outstanding from year to year. It is the fore-
going abilities which have pyramided its enviable prize lists.

Let the New Year bring a happier, healthier and
more prosperous 1966 to all!

AND
QUIETLY
GO MAD

Yours in mummery,

Joseph A. Purul
President

The last of the current Comic Clubs, the J. A. Murray New Year Association was created in 1935, by Harry W. Tyler who was made its President. In 1970 the Murray Club dedicated their participation in the Parade to Mr. Tyler, who had died in 1969 after sixty-nine successive years as a Mummer. Like most Mummer Clubs, the Murray is well represented by Mummer families; in the 1951 Parade, there were four generations of the Herman clan: Dan Herman, Sr., aged 73; Dan Herman, Jr.; Dan Herman, II; Pete Herman; Ed Herman; and Clifford Herman, 19 years old. There were also representatives of four generations of Tylers: Joseph Tyler, 76 years old; Harry W. Tyler, Sr.; Harry W. Tyler, III; Joseph Tyler, Jr.; Harry W. Tyler, II; Joseph Tyler, III; Bobby Tyler; and Jack Tyler. This club, perhaps because of its strong family tradition, tends to feature juveniles. They are the only club to list the juveniles in their copy for *The Mummers Magazine*. In 1967 they featured Mike and Scott Schults, "The Outer Space Twins," in their Parade presentation. One of the Parade marshalls in this presentation was Joseph Tyler, Jr., upholding the tradition of his family.

The Murray Club relies on current themes for ideas; in 1966 they celebrated "The Munsters," "The Flintstones," and topless bathing suits. In 1967 they celebrated mini-skirts, the "Big Blackout," and the "Men from Outer Space." In 1970 they attacked pollution. In general they place much more emphasis on floats and group presentations.

These four clubs are the current crop, proudly following the tradition as set by the clubs of the past. The Comic Clubs are the most uninhibited marchers in the Parade, and always seem to be enjoying themselves. This enjoyment communicates itself to the spectators, but above all to the individual Comic marcher. As one young Mummer put it:

> I paraded with the String Bands and the Comics, and you can have the String Bands. In the String Bands, all I could think about was playing my trumpet, it gave me no chance to think about anything else. In the Comics, I had a chance to feel the crowd. I was half tight by the time we got up the street, and then I really could sense what was going on. I could move from one side of the street to the other, and talk to people. By the time I went around City Hall, I kept thinking about the spectators: "You poor bastards, you can't celebrate the New Year this way."

This spirit, of course, is hard to judge, and the judges of the Comics have had much trouble in the past. As one judge has "confessed":

> It complicated our problem that some Mummers put on a special show for the judges, while others ignored us. There were difficult questions, too, as to whether a good idea was worth more than a well-made costume, and whether thirteen Mummers in the same get-up are funnier than five. The judges did their best, making numerous notes which they were unable to decipher when the show was over. They argued over the awards in a guarded room in City Hall, and the judge who talked most and loudest had his way. No political pressure was brought to bear on us. Nobody thanked us for our disinterested and exhausting services. It was rather nice of them, I suppose, not to throw us downstairs when the show was over and the prizes were awarded.

The best spot from which to watch the Comics is the east side of City Hall Plaza. It is here that the judges' stand is, and hence it is the target for an all-out assault. As the Shooters go "round the hall" King Momus himself takes over, and you are carried back to the Middle Ages with the Abbots of Unreason. The Band strikes up the "Golden Slipper," the Mummers begin to dance, and "piously go mad." A swirl of color springs up, waves of light, of movement, and of laughter engulf you. You become part of a great tradition.

The Fancy Clubs THE GOLDEN RIVER

When the winds blow cold up Broad Street, the Mummers suffer intensely. The great street forms a kind of wind tunnel which throws the capes of the Fancies around as if they were sailboats in a windstorm. Stately and serene in fair weather, the capes become menacing burdens in foul.

This was not always so, for the early Parades were relatively small affairs. The Shooters kept close to home, and usually wore simple costumes—the kind that could be whipped up in a hurry. Clowns, Indians, and Devils were much in evidence. A favorite costume was a greatcoat turned inside out. This continued until after the Civil War when the Shooters east of Broad Street, in 1875, organized the Golden Crown Club. Then on the west side of Broad Street a rival sprung up, the Silver Crown Club. Founded in 1875 the Silver Crown lasted longer than any other Fancy Club, marching into the 30s. It was these two clubs which brought in the Fancy Dress idea.

Following the fashion set by the two Crown clubs, in the early 80s the following Fancy Clubs were organized: William Banner, George A. Baird, Independents, Thomas Clements, Sr., Thomas Clements, Jr. These clubs were loosely organized, and many soon dropped out of competition, but not without making contributions to the tradition of the Parade. The Independents are a good example. When they took to the Street, costumes were quite simple, with none of the flaring headpieces, the widespread collars, and the flowing capes. The idea for these was conceived by Mr. Coett, founder of the Independents, assisted by his wife, daughter, and son-in-law Billy Walton. Billy Bushmeier paraded wearing a cape designed by Mr. Coett in 1880, the first cape requiring page boys.

69

This was a period of great rivalry, and the beginning of prizes for the best paraders. Money was given by local merchants; cakes and other food items were also presented to the marchers. The Thomas Clements, Sr., Club won the first cash prize in Mummer history in 1888, a prize presented at the McGowan Political Club. As the prizes grew in number, the rivalry grew. A custom grew up of the winners serenading the losers with a funeral march or some similar piece. This solicitude on the part of the winners for the losers often resulted in fierce fights. During this period the Baseler Club and the Clements, Sr., Club staged a fight that resulted in a riot call.

By the end of the nineteenth century there were many clubs, and the beginning of organization; however, the old spirit of the Shooters still shone through. A good picture of this period and the decades following can be had from the following unpublished account of the adventures of Jack Hines, a member of the Mummer Hall of Fame. In the following transcription no changes have been made in the original.

I first went out with the John F. Slater fancy club on Jan 1 1901. as an individual jockey. We cleaned up everything that year except the prize at City Hall, which was given to the Elkton club. The following year we beat elkton and won the Fancy Championship. From that year until 1914 I went out with many of the leading clubs acting only as an individual shooter and not having any thing to do with the club. I can well remember how we started the Old Timers Club. On halloween night of 1913, I had quite a few friends at my house and of course in those days you could run down to the corner and grab a "duck" of real beer for a dime. (sweet memories sez you) After several visits to the corner I put on one of my wife's wrappers and a couple of the crowd dared me to go down to the saloon with them in that make up. Of course I never took a dare, so we all repaired to Jake Kadische's "Laughing Soup" parlor where we proceeded to enjoy the evening. When we got back home some of the gang spoke of getting a crowd together for New Years Day to parade house to house. It was finally decided to hold a meeting at my home on the following Saturday Evening. I asked the boys about music. Several of them claimed they could play string instruments so I told all hands to bring their music along to the meeting. I wish you could have been at that rehearsal. One guy came in with a violin with only one string and the only one with a good sound instrument couldn't play, so I told 'em all that that line of music was out. After awhile we decided to hire a German Band you will most likely remember the German Bands consisting of about six pieces who play outside the saloons. "Nace" Ramspacher and myself was picked out to gun up the band, so Nace and I started out one evening to line up a German band for our turnout. We got tipped off that you could always land one of them bands in the neighborhood of 2nd & Popular. Well Nace and I stopped into several saloons on our way up (to look for a band you understand) By the time we landed at Second and Popular it was close on to 2 A.M. A bartender at the corner informed us that in a court down the street we could find a guy who had several such bands, so Nace and I landed up the alley which was in semi-darkness, and we gave a couple of raps on one of the doors After a while a fellow put his head out of the window and wanted to know what we wanted. I said—Have you a band? Sure I got a Band-sez he Well come on down sez I and Ill talk to you. I want to hire a band.

After a few minutes the door opened and the sleepy band master left us in.

I explained what we wanted. Six of his musicians and also a drummer. He said he could give us just what we wanted But—said I—how do we know that this band is a good band.

For answer he went to the head of the stairs and yelled
    "Hey Mike"
    "Gus"
    "Adolph"
Well you should have seen that band when they landed down stairs. They all came down in their underclothes, and they must have been sleeping with their musical instruments for every dam one of them had a cornet trombone or claranet with them. They sat down put out there music and played us all the popular airs of the day
    "Nail them quick," I said to Nace. "Give them a deposit."
We finally agreed to six brass pieces and a drummer 5 dollars per man and 2.20 extra for the leader.

We were so tickled with our band that from a group of 18 we expanded to a club of 51 members and at a later meeting we decided to enter the Broad St. parade. Boy we thought we were the works.

18 jew hod carriers in green suits. Nace Ramspacher a dutchman was Captain as an Irish Boss of the Jew Hod Carriers. A Jew drum major and a German Band. We sure thought we were sitting pretty.

Came New Years morning we had our little quarter of beer on tap at our headquarters 2341 S. Darien St. Came the cry "Here comes the band. Boy, we dragged them Heinies down the cellar and just poured the beer into them. Then I got the leader aside and asked him to get the band outside, and play the Mummers reel for the boys.

He lined his gang up and soon were listening to the sweet tune of the Wearing Of The Green. We started out Porter St. and we paraded to the tune of the Wearing of the Green. Up Broad St. around City Hall. Out Girard Ave. Down Second St. all we heard was the wearing of the Green. In those days most of the streets were paved with cobblestones, so two of the band who had "bad dogs" insisted on walking on the pavement while the other five members of the band walked in the street. My shooters amused themselves by throwing old shoes and everything available at the band, so I finally stopped the parade and told all my men to look around for a couple of cops. The leader of the Band wanted to know what was the matter. I told him I was going to have him arrested for receiving money under false pretenses.

Can't you fellows play nothing but the wearing of the Green? I asked him.

Sure—he said we can play Marching Thru Georgia

Well I said why the H— dont you play it.

All right he says

I passed along the welcome news to the boys that we were ging to have Marching Thru Georgia. The band tapped off and once more—The Wearing of the Green pealed out. One of the band got hit with a banana stork so our band for the rest of the day consisted of six men.

Finally we decided to make a stop at Claude Ramspackers at 17th and Ritner. Claude had a set out for the boys. We didnt pay any attention to the band as we had had enough of that crowd for a long time to come.

Finally when all the boys had gotten a few drinks and a little "chow" some one asked the band to play a tune. They sat down got out their music and to the amazement of the Shooters played every dam popular air of the day.

I got the leader and he explained that his band was used to standing outside saloons when they played so they couldnt read the music while they were walking so they played the only tune they could memorize hence the Irish melody. The following year we again paraded in the comic ranks and then went house to house for a number of years till Bart McHugh talked us into the fancy division where we won the Fancy championship in 1927. We went away in the hole last year when our turnout cost us close to $3000 so we decided to stay out of the big Parade this year. Several of my best shooters are working with the other big clubs and I look for the boys to make a nice showing this year.

Yours

Jack Hines

At about this time another Fancy Club was organized, the Charles Klein New Year Association. It is the oldest club in the division still participating, still performing in the Fancy Division. Founded on April 8, 1912, as an offshoot of the George W. Furnival Club, it was named after Charles Klein who was its first captain. As with the Comics, the members of the Fancy Clubs would go from club to club, and from one division to another. Clubs would spring up for a few years, and then pass out of existence. An organization would begin as a Comic Club, and switch to a Fancy Club, seemingly without reason.

A group of Mummers formerly connected with other Fancy and Comic units formed the Hog Island New Year Association on January 16, 1939. The organization was originally formed as a Comic Club by Bill "Pop" Wethman. "Pop" was a real Shooter, having been born on New Year's morning, 1869, and having paraded for seventy years. In 1951, the Hog Island Club switched to the Fancy Division and has been parading in it ever since.

The comparatively short length of time most of the Fancy Clubs have been in existence makes an interesting commentary on the history of the Parade. The average Mummers club in the old days did not retain its name long. The various groups changed leaders often, and with this change usually came a new name: hence it is impossible to reconstruct the history of many of them. Clubs exist as names only, and we cannot tell if they were Comic or Fancy. A good example of this can be had from a list of the clubs with which Frank Moir marched. Now dead, he paraded for more than sixty years with many clubs, the history of some of them unknown: Dickey Club; Mixed Pickles; Bismark; Red Onions; Stalk of Celery; Hardly Ables; Mike and Ike; White Caps;

Bruder; League Island; and Hog Island. Of this group only Hog Island, League Island, and Bruder have a discoverable history.

Today, with considerable sums of money tied up in clubhouses and other property, the Mummers' organizations are much more stable, and this trend seems to be continuing. The advent of The Philadelphia New Year Shooters' and Mummers' Association, Inc., has aided this situation also. A rule of the association is that a club must parade for five years before it is admitted to membership. The outlook, then, is that the various organizations will continue under the same leadership and charter longer now than they have in the past.

The Mummers' Association, with strong assistance from the city, sets up the rules and regulations under which the various units of the Mummers must march—there are thirty governing the Fancy Clubs. Among the more important ones are restrictions against the use of automobiles and certain musical instruments. The Fancy Clubs are permitted to use musical and imitation musical instruments other than drums, but are not allowed to use instruments that are used in a String Band. Instruments such as bongo drums, maracas, tambourines, gongs, cymbals, bells, whistles, and so on are permitted. Each Fancy Club must have at least one music band, of not fewer than fifteen men who may be costumed or uniformed, which is not judged for prizes. Each club is required to have a Captain's Cape with no more than ten page boys carrying it.

The Clubs are broken up into Brigades, each of which must have at least twenty men in costume to qualify for prizes. Two-thirds of these marchers must be over eighteen years old. These Brigades are permitted four minutes each to drill before the judges, and one point is taken off by each judge for each minute over the permitted four. The winners in the Fancy Clubs are selected on the basis of 70 percent for beauty of costume and 30 percent for presentation of theme. The club with the highest number of points is declared the winner of the Fancy Division.

Prizes are awarded in the following catagories: the Club, Trio Clown, Pantomime Clown, Captain, Handsome Trim, Juveniles, Brigades, King Jockey, Female Impersonator, Handsome Costume, King Clown, Special Mention, Trio Jockey, and

Brigade Captain. The total prize money in 1970 for the Fancy Clubs was $23,050.

Four clubs are currently in competition in the Fancy Division: Oregon New Year Association, Hog Island New Year Association, Charles Klein New Year Association, and the Golden Sunrise. In these clubs the captains' capes attract the most attention. These capes are genuine works of art, requiring considerable patience and skill for their creation. In the past great secrecy was maintained by the various clubs in order that their contribution would be a complete surprise to the other clubs. In many cases members of the same club would keep secret from each other the novel arrangements they had made to greet the new year. Several months before the Parade, every available barn and garage in Philadelphia and environs were rented to house the activities of the Shooters. These barns and garages were guarded night and day in order to ensure secrecy. In the old days a regular system of espionage was employed, each club trying to catch the others unaware and to spy upon their plans. Even today some of the clubs employ passwords to make sure that outsiders do not intrude.

In the early days of the Parade, kidnapping was not uncommon. Rival clubs would capture the captain of their enemies, and hold him until after the Parade was over. Old-timers tell tales of knock-out drops being administered to a particularly popular captain in order to keep him out of the Parade. Today there is still great rivalry but, nevertheless, close cooperation between the clubs, some even allowing rivals to use their clubhouses. This is especially common in the Fancy Clubs, for they require quite a lot of space for their creative efforts.

The customer for the Fancies must be a carpenter as well as a tailor, for the frame is usually made of wood and metal, covered with heavy silk, and trimmed with Irish lace. The frame for the King Jockey, King Clown, and Handsome Trim suits is of a fairly standardized construction. Four pieces of one-by-one lumber approximately five feet long are placed vertically so as to form a rectangle about three feet across and five feet high. These pieces are held together by four pieces of one-by-two lumber about twelve feet long, fastened horizontally to them by butterfly bolts at approximately three feet from the ground. These horizontal

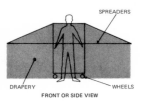

CONSTRUCTION OF A
FANCY CLUB COSTUME

SPREADERS

DRAPERY   WHEELS

FRONT OR SIDE VIEW

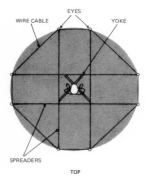

EYES

WIRE CABLE   YOKE

SPREADERS

TOP

76

supports are called spreaders by the Mummers, and rules require that they be at least six feet long, the average is twelve feet. The effect, then, is of four poles held together by four more poles fastened to them horizontally. The horizontal poles form a right angle with the vertical ones. The extremes of the spreaders are then attached to the tops of the vertical poles by eight pieces of one-by-two (two to a pole) about five feet long by butterfly bolts. Then large metal eyes are screwed into the ends of the spreaders, and a quarter-inch metal rod or cable is fed through the eyes, and soldered so as to make a complete circle encompassing the eight points of the spreaders. Four one-by-two pieces are attached to the tops of the five-foot pieces forming a square three feet across. A brace, called a yoke, is then inserted within this square, in order to allow the individual Mummer to carry it on his shoulders. This yoke may be of one-by-one or somewhat heavier lumber, and is padded at the discretion of the individual builder. It also is often the bone of contention between the builder and the man who presents the suit to the judges at City Hall. Padding is important because the suits weigh as much as eighty-five pounds, and must be carried on the shoulders of the marchers for at least three miles.

The result of this construction—and the method has been passed down from Mummer to Mummer—is of an octagonal frame, perhaps twenty-four feet around, and five feet high. The man carrying it will be able to slip under the frame, and stand up, thus lifting it from the ground. To rest, he merely stoops, and slips out from under, the suit supporting itself on its own legs so-to-speak. Wheels are optional on King Jockey, King Clown, and Handsome Trim suits, but if they are used they must be permanently attached.

The frame is then covered with heavy silk and decorated with Irish lace. Here, too, tradition and individuality merge to make for extremely ingenious costumes. The Jockey costume must always contain a horseshoe, and the Jockey must wear a Jockey cap. The horseshoes are usually in the form of a fan, their large "shoes" forming the collar. The colors are most often red and white, but all colors and combinations show up. The Oregon is famous among the marchers for its intricate use of chenille work, and its unusual color combinations. The cost of these suits varies, the average being between $185.00 and $250.00. The Individual Shooters often foot the bill themselves. One marcher in the 1968 Parade paid out $185.00 for a suit he built, but had to borrow two dollars for eating money the day of the Parade. In addition he could not carry the suit himself as he had just undergone surgery, but he got someone else to carry it for him while he went up the Street carrying the lighter suit of a Trio Jockey. So goes the life and times of a Philadelphia Mummer.

The clowns must have their faces painted as clowns, and over the years the Mummers have developed their own particular style of decoration going back at least to the days of the late nineteenth century. The clowns usually wear a white greasepaint background, with red spots on their cheeks and, generally, red streaks on their foreheads. In recent years great changes have come about in facial decoration. One-half the face might be purple and the other half yellow, or one-half red and one-half white; silver and gold makeup has also come into use.

In the Fancies and the Comics, the young Mummers are always important, but the themes of the Juveniles in the Fancies are usually more conservative than those in the Comics, featuring such topics as "Son of the Sheik" and the "Cisco Kid." The young Comics have more freedom and take advantage of it with such themes as "Frankenstein Takes a Bride," and "Just a Bum." No matter what the theme, these youngsters are always beautifully garbed, and extremely well behaved, a striking fact when we realize that some of them are only eighteen months old.

The tradition of Female Impersonator, invariably found in the Fancy Clubs, dates back to the early 1900s, when a well-known female impersonator, Madame President, held an annual New Year's Ball. The balls were all-night affairs, and the participants would usually be going home when the Parade was starting. Gradually, they formed the habit of mingling with the marchers. Today, female impersonators have become an integral part of the Parade, spending much money.

Other individuals who spend great time and money on their creations are those who participate in the battle for the most handsome costume. These individuals often attach themselves to a club, but are not really members. One man in 1968 went out as a peacock, his contribution consisting of two thousand peacock feathers mounted on a blue sequin costume. The total cost of material for the creation was $1,000; the marcher got the first prize of $325.00.

The Fancies go to great effort to come up with new themes each year. In 1970 the Charles Klein New Year Association even crossed the line, taking as their theme "The Whole World Loves a Clown."

Some of the Fancies go even farther afield. In 1970 the Hog Island New Year Association went "Around the World in Eighty Days."

> Join us as our captain recreates that epic journey around the world in eighty days.
>
> See the people of the countries that were visited as depicted by the ten page boys.
>
> See the symbols, representative of the countries as shown on the panels of the captain's suit.

The Oregon New Year Association went to the wars with "Caesar and the Gladiators." A good example of how much the Fancies give to the spectators, here is the description given by the Club:

> . . .Clad with many yards of Black and Red Velvet with Gold trim with over 1,000 white plumes will make up the Headdress of the Captain Float. Jim Young, Sr., will portray Caesar. And by his father's side, Jimmy Young, Jr., age 8, will be one of the Gladiators. This will be Jimmy Jr's ninth year parading with the Club. Once again the Oregon Club will be one of the biggest fancy clubs to parade up Broad Street. The Club will take up 20 blocks with 10 brass bands and over 23 big frame suits. And well over 1,400 New Year's Shooters. . . .

Some clubs do not like themes which are too "tight," but prefer broader presentations. The Golden Sunrise New Year Association Fancy Club chose as its 1970 presentation "The Flying Arrow." And yet within this theme, showing the Mummers' infinite variety, the Golden Crown Brigade depicted "Checkmate":

> Spectators will be amazed as Broad Street is converted into an enormous Chess Board, which will be created by the Chess pieces themselves, and each member will portray an individual piece of the 32 manned "King of Games."

78

Color and design are particularly important with the Fancy Clubs, as they must rise or fall on them alone. The String Bands depend on their drilling and music, as well as costumes, to influence the judges. The Comic Clubs rely on their antics and clever floats to catch the public eye. Therefore, the contributions of the Fancies must be made in color and form; hence, they stick more closely to the pageants of the Old World, and carry a heavier share of tradition. The String Bands represent the voice of the Parade; the Comics the eyes, seeing all and reporting, when permitted by the city fathers, to the public; the Fancies are the body, welding the Parade into one cohesive unit. A String Band covers one block, the average Fancy Club as many as twenty blocks.

The best spot to watch the Fancy Division is from a high building. From the air, on a sunny day, the Fancies are a striking sight. The great capes shimmering in the sun make Broad Street appear a golden river flowing north to City Hall, a river of warmth, of color, and of life.

The String Bands

THE SOUND COMES BEFORE THE SIGHT

The String Bands were not on hand to welcome in the twentieth century, but they missed it by only one year. The late Bart McHugh, and the late Abe Einstein suggested to John F. Towers that he lead his band in the Parade. Here is Mr. Towers' story as printed in *The Mummers Magazine* of 1948;

BIRTH OF THE STRING BANDS

(As told by Jack Towers, one of the four who originated the String Bands.)

In the fall of 1898, I was employed in one of the leading department stores in Philadelphia. Just as with the young men of today, we would meet at noon hour and discuss different topics.

One day the subject of music was mentioned. A chap by the name of John Wygand said that he played "banjo" and he, with three others would play against any four string instrument players at any time. It just so happened that I played "flute" with three others who played "banjo", "mandolin," and "guitar." His challenge was accepted and we arranged to have a "contest" to see who were the better players.

We met the following week and after tuning up, I started to play a number that the three boys whom I had with me were familiar with. The other four, instead of waiting to play their number, immediately started to play with us. That was the start and the end of the "contest." We became so interested that we played the rest of the evening together and arranged to meet every week. From time to time, new boys came to rehearsals and before the following New Year's Day, we had about 30 pieces, all string except the flute.

After two years, we were asked by Bart McHugh, who was then an entertainment promoter and who was interested in the Mummers' Parade, to go in the Parade as a novelty. We agreed.

80

Then came the problem of costume. We decided on a black face minstrel outfit. The entire cost was not as expensive as one string band captain's suit today. After three years, another string band was formed, "The Oakey." From time to time others followed.

The competition was of such a friendly nature that harmony prevailed both in music and spirit and while other instruments had been added—the sax,—accordion, bass, etc.—to lend volume, yet the string instruments predominated as of today.

This is a brief outline of how the string bands came into being. I do not want to take all the credit to myself, but being the only surviving member of the organizers, I wish to share it with my departed friends, John Wygand, William Siebert, and Louis Samuels, whose memory I cherish.

The original name of this group was the Volunteers, but this name came to a quick death at the hands of *The Svengali Show* when it played the Walnut Street Theatre. Based on George DuMaurier's novel *Trilby,* this show depicted scenes featuring the leading characters of that novel. The show was supplemented with music, and the members of the Volunteers were attracted by one of the feature songs *Alice Ben Bolt.* So affected were they by this song and the show, that they met and voted to change their name to Trilby, and it was under this name that they marched up Broad Street in their first Parade. This was on January 1, 1902. There were no provisions for prizes for String Bands in that early Parade; however, the judges awarded a consolation prize of $25.00 to the Trilby to encourage its future participation. The Trilby String Band marched in the Parade until 1921, and won many prizes. In 1935 it was reorganized by David Nelson and has been active since that time.

As it is in so many things concerning the Mummers Parade, Jack Towers' account of the founding of Trilby must be taken as only part of the story. First of all the Trilby was the first String Band to march in the official Parade, but it was not the first String Band. Before the Trilby started the tradition of String Bands in the Parade, it had been the custom of local musicians to band together into small groups and tour South Philadelphia entertaining their friends. Mr. Harry Hodgson, a life-long resident of South Philadelphia, remembered, as a very young man, seeing a group of nine musicians marching up the car tracks between Washington Avenue and Carpenter Street at Third. The year was 1894, the date January 1. These men, dressed in high hats and dusters, and wearing masks and mustaches, were playing a variety of musical instruments. Mr. Hodgson recalled a triangle, two violins, one flute, one clarinet, and a small kettledrum. The audience had to hush to hear the music. An extra touch was added by the sign they carried which proclaimed, in gold letters on a blue background, that they were the "Missing Nine." So we see that there was at least an unofficial band started before Trilby, and that this band had not sprung up quite so simply as depicted by Mr. Towers.

Further proof of this can be gleaned from the following report of Mr. David Nelson, who has spent a great deal of his life working with and for the Trilby String Band. Retired now, he was a carpenter by trade and a Mummer by choice. The story that unfolds is that of a hard-working, dedicated man to whom mummery supplied the major portion of his life outside of his job and family. Doubtless, counterparts of Mr. Nelson can be found in most of the Mummer Clubs; certainly this was the case with Joe Ferko, Billy Torelli, Joseph J. Purul, Sr., Jim Durning, and currently Peter A. Broomall, and many others; however, nowhere have I been able to find one as articulate as Mr. Nelson, nor one gifted with his memory. An attempt has been made to reproduce Mr. Nelson's pronunciation and language, for this is essentially conversation with an old-time Mummer. The interviewer's comments, italicized in the text, have been kept to a minimum.

Well, the Trilby String Band was organized really in 1900, 1900, because I have this to prove it see, the stamp. . . .I got acquainted with Lou Samuels, and Wygand in 1909, and I didn't play no instrument, so I was always interested in this here and my uncle too was. As years went by 1910 or so, eh, Wygand he was delivering ice at my house, my mother's house on Franklin Street, you know in 1910, and he said: "Why don't you get some kind of an instrument to play, a mandolin, banjo or mandolin to study?" Which I did, see, he played a five string banjo, Lou Samuels played a mandolin. So I went and took lessons for about a year, and I started to read, I made out pretty good, and it seemed like that I wasn't quite perfect enough. Because Jack Towers the musical director, he was very strict, see, you had to read music at that time, and we met at Franklin and Shunk Street in a private house, in a celler there, and he tried me out and he said: "Well, no, you won't be able to go this year." Anyway, it got to be about 19, let me see what this is, I have the picture here, it was about 19—1913, the beginning, see. So we went out as blackface Scots clan, anyway, I started from there on, and kept going right along.

And, I have to tell you how it was organized. Well, John Wygand, he had a barber shop Ninth below Moore, and it was like a clan in that section between Tasker and Moore, and they got together, what I have here is—which I know—Lou Samuels and Wygand was the originator and of organizing of it. William Siebert was in it, and Jack Towers, and a fellow named William Lester, a guitar player, was very good at that time, that I can remember. Well, they had a ladies' auxiliary they had started up in 1898, and they kept it going for two, three months about 1899 these girls, and they had a banner made for the Trilby which you can see in this picture here in the back where the horses are—you see that—well, they donated that to the band which John Wygand and Mrs. Samuels used to talk so much about it, we were at their house most of the time as kids, well, teen-agers. Yeah, they made that, so in 1900, Lou Samuels said: "I'm gonna organize a band, and I'm gonna get the stamp made." Which he did, I saw the stamp which you have proof there you see, and that stamp by the way—I did turn over to the band to Mr. Mink, and I don't know if he has it or not, but you can see for yourself, I tore it out of one of my books. Where did I leave off at there? Oh, he said he would get it organized, well, anyway, in 1900, he had this stamp made, and he was supposed to have a charter I don't know—I'll come to that later on and he had the stamp made, and that's when it got really organized, it really got organized in 1900. So, 1901 they went up Broad Street, they wore—they didn't have no costume—you would call it, I don't know just going up any old way. So they marched that year 1901, but the next year they went out, eh, —in uniform. They went out as dusters, high hats, and long coats. [*The date given for the formal entry is 1902.*]

Well, anyway, they went up Broad Street. Well, they went up for quite a few years, and there was two bands that went up; there was Oakey, Andy Oakey String Band was on Second Street right cross where Fralinger's drugstore is now, Dr. Fralinger, cross the street at Second and Segal. Well, I went up that year, and we went out in between the Fancies. Now that was the Silver Crown, or Golden Crown or either one. The band, one would go with the Golden Crown, and one with the Silver Crown, see.

So, the following year we went out as Turks. Turk suit, I can't find no picture of it nowheres. But I have it up in New York

State, I'll give it to you sometime. I'll show you, I'm dressed, playing a mandolin. Well, there was some dispute over the prize Oakey and Trilby, but Oakey beat us out of it or something or some how, see. In, in the Turk suit. Well, we, Bart McHugh was the Street Marshall at the time, and he, of course Lou Samuels was a man who was well known here and there, and around, and he must have had a store down at Second and Market, I think he had one there, I ain't sure. But Bart McHugh must have said to him, "Well why don't you take it up to the Casino Theatre at Eighth and Walnut Street?" You know, the Burlesque house up there. And he said, "One for the Trilby and one night for the Oakey String Band, and see what applause, see who would win out." Well, we went up to that, I think it was the "Million Dollar Dolls" was playing at the Casino at the time, and this must have been 1916, I think, yeah, 1915 or 1914 in there. . . .Well, they had a show down there. It was nothing to it, naturally Oakey got the money, and everything was O.K. so. Well, anyway, the name Trilby—I think I lost out on that—. . . .That's DuMar, DuMaurier's novel, yes. Well, I don't know just too much about this show here, but that's where they got the Trilby from. *Q: That was her name, Trilby.* Was in Trilby? *Q: Yes, the heroine.*

Well, anyway, in later years like about 1935, no not 1935. When Lou took the band out last in 1920, he said it was really a bad luck name. So, maybe I'm getting a little too far ahead of my, eh, story here. Well, anyway, we used to pay for all our suits, out of our own pocket, see. And the jobs we used to get we used to play up at the Blue Room at the Bellevue-Stratford. . . .Yeah, we used to play there with our suits on, and we used to divide the money up. Samuels was very good at that, a very good man, he always divided it up. Well, we played up in the Blue Room a couple times.

Well the Parade got to be fancy, it got to be fancy. . . . They got to be fancy, they got to be too much money, and we couldn't afford to, eh, pay it out of our own pockets, see. So, anyway, they used to run cake cuts, go around the streets, ya know, pick up cakes, and run the show at all, and, eh, finally we had to go and, eh, figure some other way. This here Lou Samuels, and a fellow Johnny Dryer, said: 'Well, how we go on and charter a boat." *Queen Anne* used to run up and down the Delaware, see, on a Sunday, see, sell food and drinks, and so forth, we run it down to Augustine Beach, see. So we used to make quite a bit of money to pay for costumes that cost more than we could pay out of our pocket—see what I mean? Well, that settles that, it has been going on ever since like that, you know, you have to raise money—street parties, and so forth to make money. The thing is that the fellows can't pay for those suits like, and they—our band they don't even pay dues; like the Trilby, they don't pay dues. They don't pay dues. They stopped that years ago, see.

Since, well, this was their—whatever happened here—Jack Towers he left the String Band about 1917, and joined up with the Knights of Columbus, and went overseas with them Knights of Columbus ere, and that's—seemed that's that there. I don't know what happened, he never came back with the Trilby. See, well, anyway, the band kept going until about, well, 1920 was the last of the Trilby. Cause Lou Samuels said that he would never—"You will never be able to take out the Trilby again, I'm not going to leave nobody take that name up, Trilby."

And here's a picture which you'll see Lou Samuels, and this is John Wygand. See, you don't see Jack Towers in that picture, do you? How, how about that 1916, you'll see Jack Towers, you'll see Jack Towers with the flute in the center, and you'll see Lou Samuels, mandolin. And this is Chambers, he is the one what brought out the first float for Trilby, this fellow here, he was pretty well off. . .and with the float we had a big truck, and it was a left-hand drive in them days. We went up as Romans, that year. . . .

Now, Lou Samuels had a little trouble for 1909, we didn't go up Broad Street, and he's trying to get this band over two years, which made it very bad for Lou to get them back organized again. So, I don't know, they had a fall-out with Jack Towers for some reason. I just don't know what. . . .[*Trilby went out for the next eleven years on a fairly regular basis, apparently missing only 1910 and 1911. The "fall-out" with Jack Towers, if there was one, must have occurred in 1917.*] Well, John Wygand and I—we used to go around playing quite a bit, different places—and finally I said to him "John, has Lou Samuels got a charter?"

He said, "Well, Dave, I don't know."

I said, "How we taking the Trilby again. Go on and ask him." So he asked him.

And Lou said, "Well, if you go out the right way, you and Dave could take the band out." He meant that there, we were supposed to take full charter, well, anyway, we didn't do it. Jack, John Wygand was a fellow, I don't know, he was easy going, and I was always easy going. Well, we got organized, and we went out and paraded as Wooden Soldiers, I suppose you know that, 1921, we went out. Cause that was the last, tell you what happened. We went up Broad Street, we got fifty dollar prize, and eh, eh, Lou Samuels didn't like it.

He said, "Well, this is gonna be the last. You're never gonna take it up no more," he sez, "I have the charter, ya see." Well, the band was off from 1921 to 1935, see, and naturally the Trilby, Johnny Dryer and myself always kept the Trilby name up so nobody could try to get hold of it. . . .And, well, I asked Johnny Dryer this one time, I said, "Whatta ya say we organize?" So we got organized with a couple fellows named George Boettger and his sons, and Johnny Dryer and I we organized the band in 35 again, see. . . .In 1935 we had a pretty good band organized, and we met 19th, 19th and Jackson, George Boettger's, we we had the band organized very well. Well, so Lou Samuels had got wind of it, and he had called Johnny Dryer over to his house, they lived on Cantrell Street near 22nd. Furthermore, Wygand and Lou Samuels was a boarder all them years, he lived with them see. [*John Wygand boarded with Mr. & Mrs. Samuels for more than twenty-five years, and when Mr. Samuels died, Mr. Wygand married Mrs. Samuels.*] So Johnny Dryer came, he went over to the house and he—we came back and he said, "Dave, you know you can't take that band out, because Lou Samuels has the charter."

So, I said, "Well, of Jeeze," I said, "Look at the time of the year." We had been running street parties, and so forth.

"Well, if you git," Johnny said, "If you take it out, Lou Samuels is gonna sue you, or do something you know." Well, I had to go to George McClernand, he was—I think he was president of the New Year's Association at that time, and I knew him well, because had, had been out with the Trilby, years, and I went to him.

I said, "What am I gonna do? I don't know if Lou's got the charter, we got organized we want to go up Broad Street."

He said to me, "Well, Dave, the only thing," he said, "I'll have to get a lawyer, and write to Harrisburg, and get the name changed as Original Trilby String Band." Which I gave him a hundred dollars, and he got the names registered in Harrisburg. As Original Trilby, see. Well, anyway, we, after that Lou must have got wind that I had this registered, and he never said no more, see. The band went O.K., but we had all our badges made as

Trilby, but someone said, well, George McClernand said, "You better change that, put the Original Trilby String Band on the badge." Well, this was New Year's Eve, and I had to get a stamp made somewheres in a hurry, somebody I knew, and I had to stamp all of these badges Original Trilby. Well, we went up Broad Street, and from then on it went O.K., well we went all the way up, 36 we went up, we went up as rainbows, 37 no 36 we went up as butterflys.

And the next year we went up as rainbows, and this is where Lou Samuels said it was a hard luck name. Well, we were all organized and these here Boettger, these Boettgers they—Uptown started organizing in 1937, they had six or seven fellers who was very good workers, they was raising money for us to go up Broad Street, the Trilby. They raised—they got together and made a blanket club so we would make plenty of money, see, so they were pretty good fellows. Well, they left the band, naturally there was no trouble with that, as you could always pick up four or five fellas, ya know. Well, that started it. Well, this here Georgie Boettger was captain at the time, the year of 36, Ed Quinn he was captain. It doesn't pay to have too many captains, this has been with the Trilby all these years, see. Nowdays, they have one captain and the band has been that way for years. Well these Boettgers they took the band, they split the whole band up. The fellow, a man by the name of Facenda, downtown, a real estate man, he sez, "I'll take you fellows over, and I'll take you if you go out as Young Stars." So they went out as Young Stars, well, they broke the band up, there was only about eight of us left of the Trilby October 1937, that would be the year 1938 going out.

Well, the Young Stars they had plenty of money, because a real estate man was in back of them; and we didn't have too much money. Anyway, I had to hurry up and get a few fellows together, and I didn't know who to git, it's very hard, you know in October. So anyhow, I got hold of a fellow named Ed Stewart, which was very good, I got him from eh, O'Connors String Band, or Durning's String Band I can't remember. Well, anyway, it was either one, it was a split up band too, there too, you see. Well, anyway, this here Ed Stewart came along, he was a very good man. He, in fact, if it wasn't for Ed Stewart, I don't think Trilby would ever been on the street again. I don't even say never, but I know he pulled the band out. Cause he was really, he made, he got the sketches of the suits and floats. Furthermore, I'll show you I'll show you pictures what he had done, well, for the Trilby, not for me, but for the Trilby. We had them days we had floats out, we had floats out, and he said, "You better get working, you're a carpenter," he said, "we could save a lot of money."

So, I said, "O.K., what are you gonna go as?"

He said, "What I got is minute men." So here's a picture of what will show you of what I had to go through. I had to build that float, Independence Hall, which made headlines in the *Bulletin* on New Year's Day, and we thought that we had won first prize, but we came out O.K., we came out second prize. There's another float, Statue of Liberty, now here's, eh, here's, eh, Independence Hall. That fellow sitting, sitting here, he's captain, cause I had just met him. And I said, "I'm stuck, and you'll have to help me." And he got very much interested in it, but I couldn't hardly get him to go out, well, he, so we went out as Minuets. [*He seems to have Minute Men and Minuets confused.*] So, we had a section, of course, we sent the fellows to school to teach, to dance this minuet dance, see. So, he got interested in the band, so, I'll tell you the story when later on with that, see.

And, eh, so, we went up Broad Street, and the Young Stars said to me, "Well, we're gonna run you up an alley, cause we're gone out as Three Musketeers, got beautiful suits," this is the captain you know. . . .I mean ya have fights. But you still, I don't never keep a grudge, cause that's in my blood you know Scandinavian, never try to hold, eh, he said, "We'll run you up an alley." Well we thought, cause they were beautiful suits, but we. . . .Oh, it was a beautiful set out [*Trilby's*] and the floats was two blocks long, well it made all. . . .Here's a float here, now this is our float too going up Broad Street. That's, see it?. . . .Well it was two block, and we had a town crier. *Q: Then the string bands had floats with them then?* Oh yes, well ours was that day, cause I had worked for three, pret near—*Q: No, what I mean is, did all the String Bands have floats at that time, or did?* Yea, pret near all yes, Ferko had one I got a picture in there, I can show you Ferko's that same year. We had three blocks long we had a Town Crier, everything going up, and we had a carriage from I guess you'll see it there, a carriage, and we got out from the museum.

And it seemed that the band didn't like that, it was too much money being spent. Naturally, me working and having a couple of fellas helping me, the painters and all you know, which wasn't much expense, well, anyway, it run into money. Well, two years after that, they cut this float business out, as you know you don't see no floats. . .It's like—*Q. When was that 1937 or*—Eh, eh, wait a minute, now wait. What year was that? 1938, these floats were, these here long floats. . .And so they cut the floats out, so you don't see no more floats on that there see.

But I notice, eh, Pete Broomall one year musta spent lotta money on floats, cause he had a swan, and it was beautiful. Now this man Pete Broomall, he, he worked at the Navy Yard and carpenter foreman, and, eh, he I don't know he built, I don't know who built the float for him, I wouldn't say, but, anyway, he has struggled all these years it seems he don't get nowheres neither. It seems it's bad as Trilby, eh, and I know he has hocked his home a couple of times, see.

Well, anyway, myself, I had had thousands of dollars out, myself, see. . .You know, I have to come out, well, I don't know much more now, eh, about it. Well, we took the band up, eh, and the band's been going pretty good, well its, you see he busts up that string band, George Boettger well anyway, we got it back.

Well, the war came, the band got, I'll tell you the full story. . . . The war came and we lost our whole band from there, there was nothing there. So, anyway, you know how it is in the New Year's Association, if you don't go up two years you lose out. Well, anyway, Durning was very good to me, cause we were off the street more than two years, and Durning'ed say, "Well, you gone up this year?" And, I would say, "Yes, sure we're gone up." Well, Durning always got around it some way, that he fixed up. So we was out, I don't know how many years we was out, a couple of years, two, three years. Two years anyhow, I know.

Well, anyway, this here Bill Mink he was, eh, he was, eh, with the Reddy Bell String Band. I guess you heard of them, haven't you?. . .Magistrate Reddy Bell, well they got organized. So he called me up, he had heard of me. This was in 194, eh 194, eh, eh, musta been 1940. They went up as cowboys, Reddy Bell's String Band. . . .And this is that Adam *[Adam Quaglia]* which been, was with me about eighteen years up in Gimbel's, and then he got interested, see, he, he's interested in the band now. But Reddy Bell started that band. I don't know how it is, but that first year he won second prize, with that cowboy suit. see, Magistrate Bell. So, I stayed with him for a couple of years, well, this here Adam, he didn't go up. you see, he don't play no instrument or nothing. So, the second year we still went out with Reddy Bell here, so the second year here's the second year picture, we went out as Indians, and we won first prize with that. Now Adam went up, just in the front lines dancin around, see. . .Well, when we heard this, when we heard this, up around somewheres, I don't know, up town somewheres, well, we got so excited that we won first prize. It was a rainy night, we marched all the way down from, from Second and Girard, all the way down Second Street, and I caught a cold, and I took pneumonia, and was in the hospital for two weeks. So, in meanwhile I don't know just what happened, but Magistrate Bell died, and his wife died a year after. So, that went quicker, he was a young man at that, see. But it seems so funny that how things turn out, see....And, well, anyway, I was treasurer quite a few years with the Trilby String Band, and then I turned it over to another fellow. So, Bill Mink, he was elected the president, and eh, naturally Adam was elected captain, cause he was very much interested. In back, this 19, I'd say right after the war, I'd say 45, 43, 45, 41 somewhere there....I don't think I have much more to say about it, well, oh yes, I do too, eh. I have a picture here that we were going to go out as three circus clowns, see. . . .And this is Adam and myself there. Well, Mr. Mink he says, "What do you think we gonna do?". . . .Well, he says, "Suppose we buy some, eh, buy some army goods, these here paratroops had, you know. They had different colors, and we'll make our suits."

Well, I said, "That's a good idea." Well, he wrote to Boston somewheres, and he got the figure of it. Well, I was working at Gimbels at the time, well I put in eighteen years up there, and I used to be around a good bit. And I saw these, see these clown suits which you is looking at there. . . .Well, I saw them on a rack one morning. I went up to do some work up 'ere, and I saw these clown suits, eh, eh. In Halloween right before Halloween. . . .And I saw these suits and went over to feel it, and boy it was wonderful. So, I went to the buyer, I said, "What could, how much could we buy these suits for?"

He said, "I'll have to give you a price on them."

I said, "Well, I just don't know how many it's gonna be, it's gonna be fifty or fifty-five men." Well, I give him a price, and he said, "Well, if it's, if you can pretty near guarantee that much, I think I can get it for five dollars a man." Well, we couldn't have a suit made for at least twenty-five dollars. To have it cut down all this here stuff. . . .So, we went up, five dollars, it was a rainy day you see, on that picture. . . .Well, it was a rainy day, and all these bands that really did, would beat us, we beat them way ahead, because nothing of ours spoiled, and Hegeman had this here, oh, this here glass, what-a-ya-call-it, fiber glass ya know. . . .Yes, he had suits all made of that, and it was raining, and he came way back and it was ruined. I think he would have got way ahead, but we licked him in a five-dollar suit. But you see how things turn out, for you, and we had just started back in again, and after being off the street ya know, after the war, see. . . .Well, that's about all I think I can say about this.

The above gives us a peek into the past of just one String Band. What about the others? Some are but shadows, such as the second club formed, the Oakey String Band. Founded by Andy Oakey, the owner of an oyster house at Second and Segal streets in South Philadelphia, in 1905, very little of its history is remembered. We have seen from Mr. Nelson's account that Oakey was a great rival of Trilby, and that they had a contest against each other in 1915 or 1916, which Oakey won. There are some references to it in the papers up to but not after 1918. Apparently it was a casualty of World War I.

An even lighter shadow is cast by the third club formed, the Talbot String Band. Founded by the Talbot brothers of South Philadelphia, it paraded for three years, winning three first prizes, and then disbanded. The old-timers who are left cannot remember either the first names of these brothers or their business connections, but they do recall that they were in business for themselves.

A String Band that sings as well as it plays is the John J. Fralinger, which was organized in 1914 by the late John J. Fralinger who operated a pharmacy at Second and Segal streets. At that time he had a young man working for him who was destined to become one of the all-time Mummer greats—Joe Ferko. Joe felt that starting a String Band was a good idea:

> Back in December 1914, a group of boys were standing on the corner, and we thought we would organize a String Band. Those days there were only two String Bands, the Trilby and the Oakey. So I was employed by a pharmacist down in South Philadelphia by the name of Dr. Fralinger. So, I asked him if he would buy us a banner and take us out New Year's Day, to which he consented. And January the first year that I was on Broad Street with the Mummers.

This club was reorganized in 1940 by Dr. Fralinger's son, and has been appearing in Parades since that time. Another example of a band that gets around the community, it has paraded in Runnemede, New Jersey; Collingdale, Pennsylvania; and many other towns in the Philadelphia area. Conscious of its place in the community, this organization has always been willing to parade for worthy causes and organizations.

Trilby started the tradition in 1902, and was soon followed by the Oakey and the Talbot String Bands, but things remained static for some time after that. Finally in 1916, separate prizes were established for the String Bands, or prizes were given from the Comic Club funds. This triggered a rapid fire of organizations.

In 1920 the Aqua String Band was organized by Elmer W. Leyrer, Fred J. Kesel, Sr., and nine other men in South Philadelphia. Its name offers an example of how the Parade reflects the times. The name "Aqua" was chosen because at the time of the organization of the club the controversy over prohibition was raging. Its captain at that time, Fred J. Kesel, Sr., had been parading since 1912, and was voted into the Mummers' Hall of Fame in 1959.

The glockenspiel introduced into the parade by Mr. Kesel was brought into the United States from Holland by Ernest A. Hegeman, who also started his own club in 1920. Others who helped organize the Hegeman String Band were Jack Edwards, Dick Edwards, and Bob Haney. In 1930 the band changed its name to the 69th Street String Band formerly Hegeman, with Jack Edwards as president. The club was reorganized a second time in 1933 with Albert Fink as its president, and became once more the Hegeman String Band.

The Hegeman String Band is well known for its excellent music and has won many first prizes. Two of its most popular themes were "Captain Kidd and His First Band" in 1926, and the "Roman General Troupe" in 1938, offerings still remembered in Mummer ranks. Its current musical director, Herman Seflin, joined the club in 1943, and celebrated his first year by helping the club to first prize with its theme of "Prayer for Victory." For services donated to veterans' hospitals during World War II, the Hegeman String Band was presented with an American Legion Distinguished Service Certificate. Only four of these certificates were awarded in the entire state. This is the trophy of which they are most proud, since it marks a real honor to the entire Mummers' community. This reminds us again of the special community service and feeling in the ranks of the Shooters—a spirit which is constantly making itself evident in their actions.

One of the best known and most popular of the Mummers was Joseph A. Ferko, whose band first appeared in the Philadelphia Mummers Parade in 1923. However, this band, as most Mummer bands, had not just sprung up, but evolved. Here is its genesis, as told by an anonymous writer. The manuscript, unpublished, was written in 1930, and has been cut; however, no attempt has been made to edit or correct any portion of it.

One Friday Eve—during December 1914—a group of boys were playing their musical instruments and singing the popular tunes.

As they were making merry, one of them suggested about going out "New Year shooting." However as they were too young to join either the TRILBY or OAKEY - string bands - it was necessary for them to organize their own club.

Amongst the lads sitting there was "Joe" Ferko - who suggested asking his boss Dr. J. J. Fralinger to buy them a banner in order to parade on New Years Day. The doctor consented and the club was organized namely - Fralinger String Band - and Jan. 1 - 1915 - the boys - 28 in number paraded up Broad St. with Joe Ferko as their captain. The lads were dressed in pink and blue - suit - and represented the so-called "Negro dudes."

All South-East Phila were proud of the little organization - and as they came down South Second St. - with "Joe" Ferko prancing along - they received rounds of applause. The club progressed along rapidly—and made wonderful strides - winning the championship in 1920 - attired as King's Jesters. The club paraded - 1915 - 16 - 17 - 18 - 20 & 21—no parade in 1919 on acct of war. Since then the Fralinger String Band has been dormant.

As was mentioned before - "Joe" Ferko worked for Dr. Fralinger - and after serving him for 15 years - he decided to go in business for himself - buying the drug store at the S. W. cor. of 5th & Glenwood Ave. - in 1921 -

One day a few boys came in Joe's store and asked Joe if he would captain their string band—namely the North Philadelphia String Band—organized by Otto Kauffman.

To this Joe consented - and what a bitter cold day - Jan. 1 - 1922 - It surely was one of the coldest days that the Mummers ever experienced.

93

This club returned home with Third Prize. The following October one Sunday Eve - Charles Keegan - Walter Butterworth and Joe Ferko were sitting in Curran's Restaurant 1225 Market St., and while there a discussion regarding New Years came up. Joe said that he thought he would lead the North Philadelphia String Band again. The other chaps however - advised him to organize his own club and that they would help him.

Cards were sent to friends playing string music and January 1, 1923, a big surprise was tendered the other string bands and the public in general, when the Joseph A. Ferko String Band appeared in Valentino's Toreador Costume following the topic of the day "THE SHEIK," and won second prize....

However, in 1927 - Ferko's ambition was fulfilled - and they were crowned champions - by bringing home FIRST PRIZE.

The costumes represented - "Playing Cards" were made of baronet satin. Each member wore a crown (metal) as a head-dress - studded with Jewels; - the neck piece was a ruff - white collar trimmed with gold. The capes were white and handpainted - each man representing a card—all suits - from the deuce to the ace - even the Joker was in evidence.

So we see how one club grew out of another, merged through some of its members, and then branched out on its own as the Joseph A. Ferko String Band. From its very inception this band has traveled far and wide. In its first eight years it participated in parades in Atlantic City, New Jersey; Toronto, Canada; New York City, New York; Baltimore, Maryland; Detroit, Michigan; Niagara Falls, New York; Windsor, Canada; and Cleveland, Ohio. Joe was appointed a Kentucky Colonel and was made an honorary citizen of Vermont. This club is by far the most traveled of the bands.

At about this time Philadelphia's favorite Parade was joined by one of New Jersey's favorite String Bands, the Wildwood. Here again we see the evolutionary process at work as seen through the eyes of an anonymous informant. The material written in 1930 has not been altered.

94

The history of the now famous Wildwood String Band from Wildwood, N.J. is so far a short but eventful one, and is varied in its make-up. Eight years ago a small group of men held a meeting in Harry Keatings tailor shop for the purpose of organizing a String Band as the meeting was just an improvised one for the purpose of feeling out those interested, it was decided then to make a call for players. A second meeting was called the following week with only four in attendance and the reality of a Band looked dismal. There was nothing done in the way of meetings for a few weeks, and the few who "stuck" would not listen to despair and talked string band among their friends and recruited a few more who were interested. A survey of Wildwood was made to see who could play an instrument and another meeting was called at which time seven were present with several names who said they would join. From then on the Band grew with leaps and bounds every one connected with the Band took on more energy and in three weeks they had a membership of twenty players—in May 1922 they were fully organized and made their first public appearance in a parade held by the New Jersey state Redmens convention under the auspices of the Waypolled Tribe of Wildwood—and in the evening gave a concert in the auditorium of the newly built Wildwood High School. By Decoration [Day?] of the same year the Band had now grown to a membership of 30 musicians and through the extreme efforts of Chas Heinle the treasurer the Band had secured a new complete uniform. And from then on the success of the Band was assured, and they have since climbed the ladder of fame. The following year the Band adopted the name of "The Wildwood String Band" and a more complete organization arranged with a full set of officers. The Band improved rapidly both in membership and noterity—and where-ever there was a private or public function the Band or part of it was in evidence and was well spoken and thought of by every one who saw or heard them. In December 1923 Harry Keating one of the original organizers conceived the idea to enter the String Band in the Philadelphia mummers parade on New Years'. The idea was received with a shout and from then on every one was busy. The members, their friends and the Wildwood Boosters got back of the movement and worked nearly night and day to prepare the Band for the big event. A committee was appointed to design a costume. At last all was in readiness and on January 1st 1924 made its first appearance on Broad Street—an odd coincidence was their drawing first position and lead the string division in their first turn out on Broad Street. They took the great crowds in Philadelphia by storm with 85 men in line dressed in a beautiful costume of green and white representing the typical bathing girl of the day. Cheer after cheer greeted them by the thousands of spectators all along the line which without a doubt put the Wildwood Band on the map for keeps—proof of this success was the fact the judges saw fit to award them a prize beating out two other clubs for honors. . . .In

1927 the Wildwood Band staged a scene never to be forgotten by those who saw them. This year they decided to dwell in to the past page of history and went to Rome for their idea and were dressed as the "Cohorts of Caesar" in the ancient costumes of the warriors of the Roman Empire 122 men made up the Band—and a galley of the type which sailed the spanish main proceeded them as well as two picturesque chariotts drawn by four spirited horses attended by the warrior's pages. Cheer after cheer greeted them and the applause was intense as the great crowd hailed them as the outstanding Band. The judges had a hard time to grant the prizes and only after long debate awarded Wildwood second place. This award was another rung higher for them and was considered a great honor due to the fact that at no time in the history of the great New Years parade had a Band from outside of Philadelphia received such honors. This same year found them in many important engagements due to their popularity. . .1928 again found the Band putting on a scene taken from the pages of history. This time The Wildwood Band went to China for their idea and placed before the public a costume out of the ordinary with one of the largest string band ever seen 152 men made up the Band and the color scheme was dazzeling—dressed in the ancient costume of China during the rich period of the "Ming" dynasty of the old Chinese empire of the 11th century—with a float of the temple of Budda—again the judges found it had to award their prizes and saw fit to grant Wildwood second place —weeks and months after the parade the press was still receiving letters of protest where-in they thought Wildwood should have had first. 1929 found them again displaying a costume and a story from old Russia dressed as Russian Princes of the Russian Empire in the years of their reconstruction in the 16th century. 88 men made up the Band dressed in red and gold with multi-colored plumes and jeweled head gears. Again the judges awarded them second place. This being the third time that Wildwood had received second honors during 1929 the Band again was in great demand playing at many important events. The general public was interested to such a great extent that a Radio contest was arranged to decide who was the best band. A large silver cup was to be awarded to the Winners.

The contest was held in the studio of the Columbia Broadcasting Co. and sent out through station WCAU. Wildwood Band won this contest over the Ferko Band by a vast majority thousands of letters and telegrams etc. were received from 57 different cities through-out the United States.

One of the prime movers in the Wildwood Band was Harry Keating, who was its bandmaster. One of its founders, he was an old-time vaudeville performer who had started in the Mummers Parade in 1910, and had paraded with the George A. Furnival Club, Silver Crown, Thomas A. Slater, White Caps, and Thomas Bruder—all clubs in the Fancy Division. In the String Bands he performed with the Hartmen Band and the Oakey Band before he went with Wildwood as one of its founders.

The history of Wildwood is interesting because they were the first out-of-town club to receive such attention. In talking to old-timers who saw them in action during the three parades when they received second prize, you find that the consensus is that they were "robbed," as this was in the days when prizes were not always awarded for merit. One cold afternoon, after the Ferko Band had received second prize, and complained, one of the judges patted Joe on the back and said: "That's all right Joe, your turn is next year." However, even when the judges were above reproach, the Mummers were generally poor losers or, if not poor losers, loud losers.

At about this time many more clubs sprang up in areas other than South Philadelphia. One of these in West Philadelphia was the Woodland. Organized February 11, 1926, for many years it was the only String Band in that section of the city, but has been followed by many others. The growth of the number of String Bands has resulted in a consequent geographic proliferation, and they are now found in almost every part of the city.

The Peter A. Broomall String Band was organized on March 1, 1930, by Peter A. Broomall and former members of the Wildwood String Band. Its founder and still captain, Mr. Broomall, has marched in all three divisions of the Parade and has had a most active career. The high spot came in 1960 when he was elevated to the Mummers' Hall of Fame. He has been with the Wildwood, Quaker City, and Ferko String Bands, and with the Lobster Club, M. A. Bruder, White Caps, Wyoming Hayseeds, and the Hardly Ables in the Comic and Fancy divisions.

97

Unpretentious and hard working, the Broomall String Band has been fairly consistent over the years; never in the top spot, but never in the last. Its operation is still pretty much in the hands of its first and only captain, Peter A. Broomall, who since its inception also has been its treasurer. He is assisted by three other Broomalls: James U., who is president and assistant captain, Charles, who is recording secretary, and Edward who is music director.

In costuming, this club tends to keep things fairly small. It uses precision drilling and imagination in place of money. A great deal of hand work is featured, much of it done by individual members and their families. Its 1963 theme, "The Pearly Kings of London," is a fairly typical example:

> *Costume*—Red slipper satin jacket and trousers with gold lamé cuffs trimmed throughout with Mother of Pearl sequins and large Mother of Pearl button bangles. White brocaded satin cape trimmed in gold and red sequin bangles. Red English derby. Huge backpiece representing gold crown six feet wide with all white ostrich plumes trimmed with red bangles and sequins.

For this they got fourteenth prize out of twenty-two clubs. This is some indication of their general place in the String Bands over the years—in the middle, or average group. They have risen as high as second, and fallen as low as twentieth, but they are usually found toward the middle of the prize lists.

An outgrowth of an earlier club of the same name, the Quaker City String Band, as it is known today, was organized in October of 1931. For a short time it was known as the Wildwood String Band, but soon reorganized under its old name. Under Captain Raymond Endriss, it has won many prizes and has developed strong bonds of friendship within the organization.

Quaker City is strong on family memberships. Currently there are eighteen father-and-son and nine brother combinations. There are over two hundred children in the families of the membership. This club is unique in that it is the only Mummer group to sponsor a Boy Scout troop, Cub Pack Number 731. Many other contributions are made to the community, including a party for the Police Athletic League girls. Raymond Endriss expresses this in his own way: "So many people may think a string band is only a string band. Well, it's not at all."

String Band travelers in their themes, the Quaker City has treated Philadelphia to trips to New Orleans in 1960, Spain in

1961, Ireland in 1962, and in 1963 came right out and admitted their gypsy tendencies with their theme "Gypsy Tambourines." Still doing their own thing, in 1965 they appeared as a group of traveling minstrels. Their traveling came to a stop in 1967 when they became scarecrows, the first ever depicted in a Mummers Parade. Whether traveling or fixed, however, this organization looks upon itself as a social club as well as a String Band.

The Greater Overbrook String Band, founded in 1932, prides itself on its authenticity. When it comes to correct costumes you can count on Overbrook. Over the years they have given the Parade watchers precise presentations within the limitations of the world around them. They look to the immediate and personal in their presentation. In 1965 they presented Jimmy Durante and his night club act. Here again the word "true" rings out in the Overbrook vocabulary:

> *Costume:* To present the theme of "Jimmy Durante" the band will be dressed in brilliantly colored satin costumes cut in the famous "Durante double-breasted" style with which millions of Americans have become familiar. There are eight lines of men and each line dressed in a different color, using eight colors in all.
>
> The costume will be outlined with gold sequins and topped with a white Stetson hat in the true Durante style. The band of the hat and the tie and breast pocket handkerchief will all be of one color in direct contrast to the color of the suit. Each bandsman will wear white shoes and socks to complete the costume.
>
> *Presentation:* The part of Jimmy Durante will be portrayed by our beloved Captain Harry Straub marching for his 55th consecutive year on Broad Street whose very actions and characteristics are astonishingly similar to the great Durante.
>
> The presentation will be an imitation of the night club show that Mr. Durante and his partners put on whenever and wherever they appear. The familiar Durante shuffle and his famous "Stop the music" will be in evidence as the band in response to Durante's command of "Stop the Music" will stop the music. His familiar antics at the piano will be "in the show" on Broad Street.

99

In 1970 they revived their Durante presentation in honor of Captain Harry Straub who was contemplating retirement after nearly sixty years in the Parade.

From their first Parade, the Greater Overbrook String Band has followed its first aim from the beginning—truth. The club members do research in many fields. Their 1967 presentation showed their impartiality and research. Their theme was "Mardi Gras," and they brought out a favorite rhyme used in that parade:

If ever I cease to love,
If ever I cease to love,
May the fish get legs and the cows lay eggs—
If ever I cease to love.

This rhyme, the official Mardi Gras song. is said to have been introduced into that parade by Lydia Thompson in 1870. This song was copyrighted in 1936 by Peer International Corporation. Despite its drive for authenticity, Overbrook took some liberties with the version they used.

The Overbrook String Band, even with the slight transgression with the Mardi Gras song, is versatile in ideas, original in presentation, and true to life when it can be true to life.

The Polish American String Band, organized July 7, 1933, is noted for its great spirit of competition. Especially famous for its perfectly coordinated drills, this club has won to date eight second prizes, and eight first prizes, one of the best records of all the Mummer clubs. They were the 1970 champions of the String Bands.

The spirit of this club carried over into the armed forces during World War II. Soldier-Mummers gave up Christmas leave in 1942 in order to get leave over New Year's, so that they might participate in the Parade. Forty-five of its members served with the armed forces of the United States during World War II.

They never stint with money and rely heavily on ostrich plumes for decoration. These traditional feathers of the Mummers are expensive, about $7.50 a dozen. In 1967 the captain of Polish American wore a headdress with fifty dozen ostrich plumes in it. The total cost for feathers alone was $375.00. Due to the inflationary trends of the times, the Polish American captain, Phillip Lipiecki, used fifty-five dozen white ostrich plumes in his 1968 headdress, adding turkey feathers and giant pheasant feathers. The cost of the ostrich plumes was $412.00. The money prize for the best-dressed captain of the String Bands, which was *not* won by Mr. Lipiecki, was $125.00. The Mummers have never competed for money alone, however; and the Polish American String Band Club is no exception to that rule.

The founder of the Durning String Band, James Durning, Sr., was president of the Mummers Association four different times, and was one of the strongest influences in its leadership. The Durning Club, organized on August 6, 1935, as the Thomas Connor String Band, has won two first prizes in its division. Its name has been changed several times; in 1937 it became the 48th Ward String Band, and in 1943 was given its present name in honor of James Durning, Jr., who was at that time serving overseas as a sergeant in the army.

James Durning, Sr., was in politics, and served as the chauffeur for Philadelphia Mayor Barney Samuels for many years. His involvement in mummery and politics produced some memorable moments, as we shall see in the next chapter. Always a practical politician and organizer, Durning kept close control of his club, and today it is the only Mummer organization which carries the business sign of approval "Inc." after its name.

Partly because of the practicality of this man, his club became an example of how the Parade could publicize and carry its name far and wide. It has appeared at many important events, among them the Atlantic City beauty pageant, Madison Square Garden boxing shows, Allentown's Halloween parade, and the Washington-Eagles football game at Washington, D.C. Everywhere this club has gone, the name of the city of Philadelphia has gone with it, and the city has received good publicity of an extremely worthwhile nature.

A club which believes in performing a real community service is the Uptown String Band, organized in February of 1937 by George Beiderman, Warren Runkle, Tom Walsh, and Robert Runkle, Jr., who has been its captain since 1939. Mr. Runkle now shares his duties with a co-captain, Ernest Jacobi, as he has been suffering from multiple sclerosis for many years. Despite this handicap, he has always appeared in costume to greet the spectators. In the past he has been led, in 1970 he rode in an automobile. This kind of drive, typical of most participants, is also found in community activities of the Uptown String Band. A believer in the idea that a Mummer club must be part of the community, the Uptown has always taken an active part in area projects, and for many years has held classes in its clubhouse. The members are known in their neighborhood as "ambassadors of good will and good fellowship."

This club uses costume material with a great sophistication and understanding. In 1963 it paraded with the subject "Waltz Theme." The attention to cloth texture is obvious:

> *Costumes:* Jacket—Colonial design of white moire in square cut fashion. The moire is an effective luxury woodgrained effect, encrusted with organza lace embedded with gold motifs and jewels.
>
> Vest and britches—Consists of Lavender Moire to accentuate the whiteness of the jacket.

Uptown placed consistently between eighth and twelfth in the prize list until 1957, when it got first place with its theme "Syncopated Clock." This costume featured headpieces with clocks which actually worked. The cost of the clock mechanism for each costume was $80.00; multiply this by sixty, the number of bandsmen, and you get $4,800.00. This does not include the cost of the material and plumes, nor of the costumes themselves. One estimate, that of an anonymous member, put the total cost of the presentation at $10,000. The first prize that year was $2,000.

The Avalon String Band was organized on May 11, 1938, by Harry T. Lawson, still its captain and treasurer. The organization paraded under the name of the 12th Ward String Band from 1938 to 1943. In 1944 it changed its name to Avalon, and has been marching under that banner ever since.

Another "average" club, Avalon has a long history of modest successes, with an occasional home run. In 1947 it paraded with the theme "The Crusaders," making a plea for racial and religious tolerance. That year it featured the hymn "Onward, Christian Soldiers." This is an example of a new morality play, and a contribution to mass communication which adds a grace note to Mummer history. Here is the manifestation of the voice of the Parade asking for the help of God in solving man's problems; a voice, sincere and direct, speaking for all people. For this contribution it received sixth prize and $850.00.

The Duffy String Band is a comparatively new club, having been organized on March 4, 1945. Originally called The Fire-Fighters, it was created at Engine Company Number 22, 214 Pine Street, Philadelphia. Its members at that time were all Philadelphia firemen or auxiliary firemen. The originators of this group were George E. Duffy, John Lauria, Harry Y. Dittmer, Salvador Manganero, and Edmund Burk. George E. Duffy, a battalion chief in the Fire Department, was chosen its first captain, and served in that capacity until his retirement in 1959.

The Fire-Fighters changed their name to Duffy in 1951, and in that year captured sixth place in prizes, the highest they had ever placed. In 1952 they dropped to fourteenth, and apparently got discouraged, because they remained out of the 1953, 1954, 1955, 1956, and 1957 Parades. Despite the String Band Association's rule that a club that remains out two years is dropped from membership, they returned to action for the 1958 Parade, with Henry J. Kunzig, Sr., as captain. Again they got fourteenth prize.

The history of this club might serve as a capsule account of the typical Mummer club. We have seen it in detail with the Trilby String Band, now we see it in a recent club. The pattern runs generally like this: The originators get old and discouraged by losses; new blood comes in and pushes the old leaders out. Much of this struggle goes on under the surface, and continues and compounds until a strong leader emerges to hold the club together. With Trilby it was Dave Nelson in 1932, with Duffy it was Henry J. Kunzig, Sr., in 1958.

In 1959 George E. Duffy retired. Today this kind of struggle still goes on, not only inside individual clubs, but in the String Band Associations as well. We will discuss this in relation to the String Band Association in our next chapter, but for the time being, the Duffy String Band history might serve as a kind of microcosm of Mummer inner conflict. The conflicts usually remain unknown to the public and generally do not affect the Parade.

Young and aggressive, the South Philadelphia String Band, founded by Sam Hamilton, Sr., May 14, 1946, has an enviable record and reputation. They have served as honor guard and escort to Governor Hughes of New Jersey on that state's July 4th celebration, and they have performed at the Barnum Festival in

Bridgeport, Connecticut. Known as "The Fabulous S.P.S.B." they are proud of their outfit, and not afraid to say so. They feel they have earned their reputation as "Always a favorite on Broad Street," and in most of their publicity they make sure the public knows this. Their captain, James Donaghy, is the only String Band captain to have won three consecutive Best Dressed Captain's prizes.

Their ego spills over into their Parade themes. In 1966 they won first prize with their theme "String Band Hit Parade." Young as they were, they decided to "show" the other bands what the "real" String Band sound was like.

> Our Costume Committee, after many hours of discussion arrived at the conclusion that the Mummers String Bands were getting farther and farther away from the music and traditions of our origin, with more and more accent on Classical and even Light Operatic music.
>
> Therefore, they decided to try and revive the "Real" String Band sound and designed a costume to carry out the theme of some of the "ALL-TIME" String Band songs, such as "Four Leaf Clover," "Alabama Jubilee," "Heart of My Heart," "Sunny Side Up." "Oh Them Golden Slippers," etc. The Cape, Trousers and Tunic will be of White Brocaded satin and an imported French Metallic Black Iridescent Brocade, elaborately trimmed with many yards of white lace, and ornamented throughout with Hearts, Golden Slippers, sunbursts and so on, all made of Sequins, Gold and Silver Lamé and high-lighted with simulated jewels. A towering four foot tall hat will carry white and gold Ostrich plumes. Peacock "Eye" feathers, and other exotic bird plumage from all over the world, even our shoes will recall the "Good Old Days" as they will be laquered in brilliant gold.

The best part of the story is that they were successful in creating the atmosphere of old, and the strings never sounded better on Broad Street.

The Greater Kensington String Band was founded in 1948 in early October, and is another good young club. It too has had its victories and defeats, but one word that runs through their statements to the public is "proudly." Their themes sometimes reflect this feeling:

The Greater Kensington String Band proudly presents their 1966 Theme, "The Vanishing American," and recalls the story of this great council. In their presentation you will see one of these great tribes leaving their hunting grounds for a new life. You will see Chief Nufonot lead this exodus escorted by Tom-Tom drummers. You will watch these many chiefs form a living Totem pole as they bid goodby to their land. Prouder days are recalled as they perform a traditional Indian war dance in interlocking circles.

For this presentation they received second prize, for the third time in their history. They have never won first prize, but are extremely optimistic about their chances. Even water cannot dampen their spirits.

Incidentally, you may remember the G.K.S.B. as the band that was "sunk" while on board a raft at a water carnival in 1963, losing many of their instruments, and ruining a large portion of their costumes. However, as you watch the G.K.S.B. presenting their 1964 theme, you will certainly see a string band that, "Ain't Down Yet."

Energetic and proud, the Kensington Club has a lot of great history ahead of it as well as behind it.

This then is the story of the "official" String Bands participating in the Philadelphia Mummers Parade. However, as it is in almost all matters touching the Parade, this is only part of the story. Sixteen of the clubs are official members of the Philadelphia Mummers String Band Association, a closed corporation. In order for a club to get into this association, it has to donate $10,000. to some charity. This serves as a deterrent to expansion of the association and as a handicap to other competing clubs.

The official organization makes it possible for the member clubs to make considerable money from their annual presentation of the "Show of Shows" at Philadelphia's Convention Hall. The String Bands perform seven shows in February. Admission prices range from $2.50 to $4.50, and the individual clubs split the profit. Clubs not in the association must find other ways of financing and this is difficult.

In addition, the periphery clubs are excluded from the annual *Mummers Magazine,* published by the Philadelphia New Year Shooters' and Mummers' Association Inc. This magazine is sold on the streets during the afternoon of New Year's Day for $1.00, and the association gets the profits. This hurts the outside clubs, because the spectators are not able to learn in advance who they are or what their themes are to be. Hence their battle is up-hill all the way, but they have managed to make their strength felt in many ways, including winning several first prizes.

There are six unofficial String Bands, the oldest is the Dick Crean, founded in 1947 by Mr. Crean. Their record has been fairly inconspicuous, although for a brief period they were among the first four prizewinners. In 1953 they placed fourth with "The Wheel of Fortune," perhaps an ironic indication of how they felt about their chances in bucking the system. In 1955 they reached third place with "Sunrise," but went rapidly down the prize list thereafter. They have, over the years, battled hard and will continue to battle to reach the top. Perhaps a good omen is their new captain's penchant for high headdress. In the 1967 parade, Captain Frank J. Beatty, marching in his second Parade as leader, wore on his shoulders a Dutch Windmill fifteen feet high and thirteen feet wide. As he had to dance before the judges wearing this dress, it took great strength and finesse, so perhaps more will be heard from the Dick Crean Band in the future. In 1968 they changed their name to Dick Crean (or the Rising-Sun) String Band, so perhaps once more they will see their sun rise higher in the winner's ranks.

The Ukrainian American String Band, founded in 1949, has specialized in rather small, intimate productions over the years. They stress individual performances, such as dancing, and group presentations. The problem of financing has haunted them as well as the other unofficial clubs. In 1955 and 1956 they did not participate in the Parade, but came back in 1957 with a simple but picturesque presentation, "The Gay Nineties," for which they got sixteenth prize.

In 1965 the underdogs really hit the other clubs where it hurts, by winning the first two spots on the String Band Prize List. The Ukrainian American contributed to this victory by capturing second prize with a most unusual entry for a Mummer group

"The Anointment of King Solomon." Two things stood out about this contribution: its dignity and its authenticity. Their Captain, Barney Steegmueler, dressed as King Solomon, wore a white velvet, silk, and satin shawl trimmed with rhinestones and brilliants. They marched quietly and in character the entire route of the Parade, and before the judges stand performed the rites of an anointment, and then selected dancers danced the Hora. This was by far the most unusual presentation for a Mummer group this author has ever seen.

Members of the Jewish ethnic groups do not as a rule participate in the Parade. Occasionally a few individuals participate, but there usually is no representation of Jews as a group. The members of the Ukrainian were not Jewish, but did work with Jewish friends to keep within the tradition as best they could. It was touching to see the large Star of David headdress worn by the individual bandsmen. The music they played was likewise outside of the Mummer tradition: "Land Flowing with Milk and Honey," "Hope of Building the Temple," "Evening in the Garden," "Out of Zion Shall Come Knowledge," and "Let Us Dance a Hora."

In 1966 and 1967 they dropped back on the prize list, but pleaded in 1968, as "Prisoners of Love," for one more chance. It is obvious that this club will have many more chances for prizes on Broad Street and to spread a kind of tolerance not always found in Mummer ranks.

The club which won first prize when Ukrainian American won second, for a grand slam, with the Greater Bucks County String Band, founded by Frank Weller in 1949. Mr. Weller still heads the club he founded, and this continuity and his leadership has made this the most successful and important of the clubs outside of the Mummer organization. Off to a slow start, apparently at times marching under another name, they first show up in the winning records in 1955 in seventeenth place with their entry "Sweethearts on Parade."

After this they began a steady rise in the standings: 1956 fourteenth, 1957 and 1958 thirteenth (they seemed to have a penchant for thirteenth as they won it four times over the years), 1959 third, and then in 1965 the top spot with their "A Hawaiian Holiday." Their Captain, Frank Weller, also won first prize for the Best Dressed Captain that year. There is an ironic note in this event, his name was spelled Feller in the newspapers. This was because the reporters did not have access to the same information on Weller as they had on the other captains whose clubs were listed in the official *Mummers Magazine.* This day Ed Venckus, of Aqua, won second place, and Phil Lipiecki, of Polish American, won third. Both their names were spelled correctly, but that was not to be with Weller.

Captain Weller's costume featured a six-foot high headpiece with 420 ostrich plumes, two torches, and a Polynesian mask, outlined by vulture feathers. His bandsmen wore bright-colored Hawaiian shirts and silk trousers trimmed with gold. In their plumed headpieces, they wore orchids. Before the judges they performed an intricate native dance.

Quite often they feature items of fantasy in their themes such as: "Disneyland," "The Great White Way," "Indian Fantasy," and "A Tribute to Emmet Kelly." In 1966 they received fourth prize, in 1967 were back to thirteenth, and in 1968 up to ninth. Perhaps they are once more on that road back.

A persistent club is the Garden State String Band, founded in 1949. Most of the unofficial clubs have dropped out of the Parade for a year or two in their existence, but not Garden State. They started off their Parade career earning thirteenth prize, and placed higher than this only once —in 1955 they placed eighth and their Captain, James King, won third prize that year as Best Dressed Captain.

The Palmyra String Band paraded its first two years without a prize, then it took eighteenth prize out of twenty in 1951, only to go back to "no prize" in 1952. This club is a good example of the underprivileged, fighting for its life. Together with Harrowgate, founded in 1950, they share the same problem: survival. In 1965 they had to drop out of the Parade. James Smart in his column "In Our Town," in *The Evening Bulletin* of Tuesday, December 8, 1964, explains the situation:

> But the string bands are perhaps the ultimate in Mummery—more organized more lavish, more serious in their efforts to present a pageant of which the city can be proud. And more expensive.

> And so the Palmyra String Band and the Harrowgate String Band dropped out this time.

Anthony D'Amato, the Palmyra captain, and Harold Trievel, the Harrowgate captain, both say they'll be back in the next Parade. They have to say that. If a band misses two consecutive Parades, the Parade rules eliminate it permanently.

The setback to the Harrowgate band hits me personally. That's my old neighborhood. Harold Trievel lived right around the corner from my family.

I asked him what the probelm was.

"Lack of funds and lack of interest," he said.

Not enough musicians were showing up for rehearsal. Expenses went up at their rented headquarters. . . .

D'Amato's problems in Palmyra are the same.

The story did have a more-or-less happy ending, however; both Palmyra and Harrowgate marched in the 1966 Parade. Palmyra placed last of twenty-two clubs, and Harrowgate placed fourteenth.

One characteristic phrase comes up often in the papers when they describe the unofficial clubs; that is, "In his first year as Captain." There is a great turnover in leadership in these clubs. The best one is the only one with its original leader, the Greater Bucks County with Frank Weller. Two factors seem to work together, strong leadership and money—when a club has strong leadership, money is easier to come by. Without leadership, money alone will not make a great club but it is necessary.

Along with the String Bands marching today about which we have read, go a whole group of "shadow clubs." These are organizations which once marched, but do so no more, and their history is lost. You come across their names in old newspaper accounts of winners, but no one seems to remember anything about them. One of the earliest clubs of this type is the Talbot String Band, which won first prize in 1916, 1917, and 1918. From Dave Nelson we have learned that the club was formed by two brothers by the name of Talbot who were businessmen. The rest of its history is missing. We also know a little about the Oakey String Band again from Mr. Nelson. However, the other clubs are just names. Here are some of the old clubs, and the years they paraded: Aronomink, 1921; North Philadelphia, 1922-1925; Trixie, 1922-1933; Beach Progressive Club, 1923; Steubing, 1924-1928; Franklin, 1924; Dixie Serenaders, 1925; Lawndale, 1926; Octavius V. Cato, 1928-1929; Golden Slipper, 1933; J. J. Morrow, 1935; McCracken, 1935; Hegemen-Lancaster, 1936; Milton Rose, 1936; J. J. Morrow, in a return 1936-1938; Dickson, 1936; Rogers, 1936; Greenwood, 1937-1942; Dixon? (should it be Dickson?) 1938; Young Stars, 1938-1941; Belmont, 1938; Feltonville, 1939-1941; Whitman, 1940-1943; South Jersey, 1940; 38th Ward, 1941-1943; 35th Ward 1941-1942; Bell, 1941-1942; 26th Ward, 1941; Myers, 1942; Bill Morrows, 1943; 25th Ward, 1943; 5th Ward, 1943-1944; Northeast, 1948; Delaware County, 1948; Frankford, 1950; Mayfair, 1950; Penndel, 1951-1953; Tinicum, 1953; Crescentville, 1957.

Upon looking over the preceding list of shadow clubs, one must admit that some throw strong shadows. Trixie for example performed for eleven years, winning third prize in 1925, but the average existence appears to be three years. Why this plethora of paraders is a question difficult to answer. With a few individual clubs some clues emerge. Reddy Bell organized his club in 1941 and died in 1942 after winning first prize. Some other clubs merged with existent clubs, and so lost their identity. The Octavius V. Cato Club dropped out in 1929 after two years of parading; legend having it that they dropped out because they got last place. This club was the last Negro String Band to perform in the Parade. That their dropping out coincided with the Depression leads me to believe that they dropped out because of financial reasons. In reading Dave Nelson's story we get some information on the Young Stars. They were drop-outs from Trilby, and were sponsored by a real estate man by the name of Facenda. When one man sponsors a band, often the other members do not work as hard to raise money, and after a few years the sponsor gets tired, and the money stops and so does the band. This happened with the Young Stars.

Whatever the reasons for the large number of bands, the fact of their existence is intriguing. I have been able to get fairly concrete information on twenty-four bands, and yet there are forty-three more about which little is known. That totals sixty-seven String Bands that have functioned in this city since 1901, at least those I have been able to track down by name. There must have been more of which I have found no mention. The tremendous vitality and mobility of individual mummers in the String Bands is a good indication of the hold the Parade has on the citizens of Philadelphia.

What is the source of this fascination? Why did you join a String Band? Here are the answers given by six members of the Ferko String Band.

Joseph Ferko, Captain: I got interested in String Bands while a student at the Philadelphia College of Pharmacy. In 1923 I organized my own String Band. My boys and I have entertained millions since. I'm happiest when strutting in a Mummer's Parade.

Harry Leary, President: The day I met Joe Ferko. I listened to his band rehearse and said, "This is for me." I've been with Joe 35 years. My biggest thrill was appearing with Jackie Gleason. He went crazy over the music, strutting and singing through rehearsal.

John Gilbert, glockenspiel bells: String Band music fascinated me as a child watching the Mummers Parade. I took music lessons. My aunt Carrie knew Mr. Ferko and arranged an audition. I was a happy kid when I made the band ten years ago. I was thirteen.

Richard Wojczak, accordion: My love for music. When you're 16, like I am, and belong to a famous band like Ferko's you feel important. When I parade up Broad Street, I feel like an actor on stage. I love the crowd and applause.

Charles Wagner, mandolin: I joined for good fellowship. Joe Ferko is wonderful. Our town takes its String Bands for granted. Out of town they go crazy when we entertain. We are guests in their homes and they are still cheering when we leave.

Harry C. Teller, guitar: For fun. It is wonderful to watch people enjoy themselves. Our music makes them want to sing and dance. The expressions on youngsters' faces are wonderful. I get a big kick out of watching them as we parade.

One fascination with the String Band musicians stems from the personal involvement necessary for success in presenting their numbers. In the Fancies and Comics, men work together, but one man cannot upset the whole production. This is not so in the String Bands. Here, individuals are less important than the team.

III

Fellowship is obvious in the String Band clubs, it makes itself evident in the rehearsal and in the performance. Most decisions are made by the group for the group.

In the Ferko Club the members help design the costumes. A basic theme is decided on, then a member models it for the entire organization. For the 1964 theme, "The Three Musketeers," the costume was a doublet of twill-back velveteen. The basic color was wine red, and the auxiliary color silver. This costume required a waistband, and the membership decided what color that band was to be. The model stood on a table, and the individual members commented, and offered improvements which were taken into consideration and debated. "Why not try an orange band?" a member would shout, only to be answered by another, "That would clash, how about purple?" And so it would go, until the decision was made.

The type of action goes over into the music as well, the bandsmen discuss all elements with the music director, and arrive at music decisions democratically. The fellowship of the individual clubs makes this possible. There are arguments and disagreements, but in general good fellowship prevails where costumes and music are concerned.

Currently there are twenty-nine rules governing the String Band activities in the annual Parade. Sixty-four members is the maximum number in a band. The music is arranged, and the majority of the musicians read music. Eighteen men marched in line in 1902, the first Parade in which the String Bands participated. String instruments predominated in early bands; later flutes and saxophones were added. The basic instrumentation was guitar, mandolin, banjo, and violin; but when the need for greater volume was felt, clarinets, saxophones, and accordions were introduced, followed by the glockenspiel. The Hegemen String Band is given credit by the old-timers for having introduced the saxophones into the Parade. Accordions were introduced sometime around 1925; up to that time there had been separate accordion bands. In 1925 there was only one accordion in the Ferko Band but today there are ten or more. In the early thirties there were very few saxophones; today they dominate the average String Band. This growth has caused an extraordinary combination of instruments: violins, bass viols, banjos, clarinets, saxophones, drums, guitars, mandolins, glockenspiels, and guitar-banjos.

This requires some very difficult work for the arranger. Here is part of an interview by Joseph P. Barrett with William Conners, then music director of the Ferko String Band.

. . .On modern songs, he said, he or his assistant Bob Traub, make an arrangement from a piano copy.

Sometimes, for special arrangements, the band takes the piano copy to a professional arranger.

An arrangement is made in three-part harmony for first alto, tenor and third alto saxophone. Also, for violin, and two bass parts, a string bass and a saxophone bass.

Included in the arrangement is a lead sheet for banjo, guitar, mandolin and accordion. . . .

No Written Music for Some.

Some of the songs that we play, such as "Pasadena" or "Scrap-iron" have no written music.

"Scrapiron" is a well-known old Mummers' number commonly attributed to Jack Towers, who has been a Mummer all of his life. I knew this song by heart and went to our arranger and hummed it to him.

"He put the song down on paper and then arranged it."

Another important point, made by many Mummers, is that competition is great, each band trying to outdo the others. This has caused a change in tempo from the past. Now the battle cry is "drive." Jim Durning, then leader of the Durning String Band, is credited with the statement, "I don't care how well you play, how loud can you play?" The tempo of the bands is, thus, much faster today than in the past. This increase started after World War II, according to Johnny Gilbert, Historian of the Ferko String Band.

The old-timers complain of this "driving" but go along with it. In the main they try to maintain both drive and quality in their music. It is felt by the Shooters that the Kensington String Band is closer to the past than any of the other clubs.

Violins are played in an orthodox manner; and a rounded bridge, all of the bow, and all positions are used. Most of the instruments are tuned on the accordion, as this instrument does not change its tone outdoors or because of a change in the temperature. Saxophones play an important part in the bands: their ratio to other instruments is one to four, sometimes one to six. All makes are used and all keys are played, although C, F, B-flat, A-flat, and G are most popular. Bass viols, usually about three to a band, are plucked and bowed.

Steel-stringed banjos, generally in a one-to-four ratio to other instruments, are also prominent in the band and are stroked. The old-timers are proud of playing them in the coldest weather without gloves. They use a combination of camphor-ice and Vaseline to protect their hands. No steel guitars are used, and regular guitars are losing favor since they produce little volume and any type of amplification is forbidden.

Although only two glockenspiels are used in a band, their importance lies in the fact that the Mummers consider it the instrument that gives the band its sound. Usually eight standard accordions, one bass drum, and one snare drum are also included in a band.

This combination, from a folk-music standpoint, is interesting. The unique features are the combinations of the instruments, and the fact that the music is played outdoors while the musicians are marching (the tempo is almost always march time).

The music has gradually changed over the years. Acceleration of tempo has increased a great deal, and the strings have become less important. In the early days the music was selected for its individual theme. Today things are different. For example, in the 1964 Parade the Peter A. Broomall String Band presented "A Musical Tribute to Johnny Appleseed," using a most elaborate costume of apple green and white slipper satin trimmed with red apples edged with sequins. Each Mummer had a cape trimmed with a large red apple in the center, with smaller apples on the sides. Johnny Appleseed's apple bag was made of gold basket-weave lamé with red satin straps. The headgear consisted of forty light green plumes on top of gold tree trunks outlined with black sequins. The musical numbers supporting this presentation were "In the Shade of the Old Apple Tree," "Apple Blossom Time," "Don't Sit Under the Apple Tree with Anybody Else but Me," and other "apple" songs.

The trend toward an individual theme has brought about an interesting revival of the mimetic impulse. Now the bands are judged 40 percent on music, 40 percent on costume, and 20 percent on presentation or drill. In the fairly recent past, music had counted at least 70 percent in the judging, and still earlier 100 percent. Thus, the circle has been completed, from mumming to music to mumming.

A survey of fifty years of prize winners among the String Bands mirrors the popular taste in music in those years. In the 1920s in Philadelphia, according to one informant, the Parade was literally the Hit Parade, the easiest way for the populace to learn of the most popular songs and the latest fads. The Aqua String Band, named in honor of prohibition, won first prize in 1922 with the theme "The Kewpie Dolls"; Ferko won second prize in 1922 with the theme "Rudolph Valentino," and in 1925 won second again with "Mah Jong." American Indians have been the most popular Parade figures over the years: legend has it that no Parade has ever gone up the Street without them, a distinction which only "devils" can match.

One of the most important elements in the modern Parade is the Mummers' theme song, "Oh! Dem Golden Slippers," written in 1879 by James A. Bland, a Negro, and composer of over 700 songs, including Virginia's theme song, "Carry Me Back to Old Virginny." The public is told that "Golden Slippers" is an old Negro spiritual; in fact it is a satire on the Negro spiritual. An advertisement for it on the back of the first edition carries this statement: "One of those ever popular negro melodies, which never fails to convulse an audience with laughter." The cover of this original sheet music is quite anti-Negro. It consists of two musical-comedy-type Negro caricatures, attended by three black crows.

"Oh! Dem Golden Slippers" joined the Parade in 1905 when Charles Dumont, an old-time minstrel man, used it for several marching clubs. It is by far the all-time Mummer favorite in the String Band's repertoire. Today, this piece is synonymous with the Parade, and the golden slippers of the angels have been transferred to the Shooters. This musical piece is played by every String Band that goes up Broad Street, and is the one number that has never grown stale. It has basic rhythm with simple harmony which lends itself to the dancing of the characteristic Golden Slipper or Mummers' Strut.

The variations of the Mummers' Strut are almost as many as there are Mummers. The youngsters do a rather straight-up Strut, generally carrying opened double or triple parasols which they move up and down in rhythm with the music. Using a hopping gait, they take one step forward and a half step back, repeating this five to seven times and then spinning around from left to right; they repeat this procedure as long as the music is played, usually a minute and a half. Although this step may sometimes be danced to other music, it is always danced when "Oh! Dem Golden Slippers" is played.

Each String Band captain has his individual Strut. The most famous was that of the late Joe Ferko, known by the Mummers as the "dancing captain." It was he who started the custom of Mummer captains dancing in front of their bands. Joe followed the usual full step forward, half step back, but instead of spinning at the end of his first series, he made a turn and came back, using the same step back. At the end of his five to seven steps back he spun from left to right in a kind of curtsy, holding the front of his cape or costume; he then went forward again, using the full step forward, half step back. During his dance he did not straighten his knees or his back. He held his head up, but the general impression was that of an Indian doing a war dance to a very slow tempo. The interesting thing about Ferko's Strut is that the bent-knee stance was accidentally innovated by a temporary physical infirmity. During one of Ferko's early Parades, his knees had locked in a bent position when he had been sitting on the tailgate of a truck, resting. When he got out of the truck to lead the band, he could not straighten his knees, and thus had no choice except to dance with his knees bent. This style caught on with the crowds, and he danced this way in every subsequent Mummers Parade until his death in 1964.

Occasionally the numbers of the String Bands catch the national pulse. One such was "I'm Looking Over a Four-Leaf Clover." This song, composed in 1927 by Mort Dixon and Harry Woods, had been quite popular in 1928, and years later became what is known in the music trade as a "sleeper." Captain Robert Runkle of the Uptown String Band picked it in 1948 to be his unit's theme, and worked in a vocal number for his band to sing as they played. A popular band leader Art Mooney, caught it up and, on a national network, played it as the String Bands did. It took the nation by storm. Day and night it beat upon the ears of a defenseless public. Sensational numbers of records were sold and public interest continued for many months but, finally, like the old soldier, it faded away. This has been by far the most successful of Mummer numbers, and has helped popularize the Parade on a national level in addition to raising some money for the String Bands. However, a great deal of the money earned by this number went to the record companies. Several small companies sprang up, made contracts with the Mummer String Bands, cut a few records, made a killing, and then went bankrupt.

Not all Mummer pieces are so sensational, however. Some are slow steady numbers which keep reappearing over the years, retaining their popularity with the public. Two such numbers are "Scrapiron," and "Honey Boy," both attributed to Jack Towers, who seemed to have a feel for Mummer music. These melodies were composed especially for the String Bands and are the most typical of all Mummer musical arrangements.

As the String Bands grew more popular, their ranks enlarged and their versatility increased. At first the costumes were simple, usually consisting of high hats and dusters; gradually they became more elaborate and costly. Today, the costuming of the String Bands is very important, and it is put on an equal basis with the music for judging, 40 percent for each. The other 20 percent is for the drill, which has improved greatly over the years. The first String Band, Trilby, contented itself with simple close-order drills, but this is no longer the case; today, along with development in costuming, has gone an equal advance in drilling and originality of theme. Many of the themes in recent years have been genuinely artistic, and have revealed an excellent conception of design and color harmony.

With this overall improvement in music, costuming, and drill, has come an increasing popularity with the public. In 1951 the Philadelphia *Evening Bulletin* took a poll of the city of Philadelphia to determine what Division of the Parade was most popular with the public, the String Bands were picked by an overwhelming vote. The results were as follows:

Division	Percentage of People in Favor
String Bands	58
Comics	16
Fancies	12
Floats (separate from divisions)	4

(Since some persons named more than one section, the percentages do not add up to a hundred.)

In 1968 an informal poll taken by the author on the Street during the Parade, showed that over 75 percent of the people favored the String Bands over the Comics and Fancies (155 out of 200).

The String Bands have grown from a few scattered groups in the early 1900s to many highly organized clubs. Today, the numbers have increased and the quality has steadily improved. The music has developed into a unique style, a style that is particularly expressive of the spirit of the Shooters. It is down to earth, made up of simple melodies and lacking complicated chords. George F. Kearney, a long-time Mummer buff says of the Mummer music:

> Some day it will be recognized that Mummers' music is just as interesting as modern swing and calypso. This music of Mummery played by our present String Bands has a distinctive seductiveness, a "Folksy" quality meriting further study and attention.

This music has more of an up-beat than is usually found in nonclassical music, and it is this quality that seems to give it its personality as much as anything else.

The best place from which to watch and hear the String Bands is the East Plaza of City Hall. This spot is always the most sought after, as the Clubs expend their greatest efforts before the judges' stand which is erected there. The Plaza serves as a sounding board for the music, and a frame for the drilling. This combination makes a complete picture, satisfying the ear, the eye, and the heart; a picture which is renewed each year early in January in Philadelphia.

DON'T RAIN ON MY PARADE

It is nearly impossible to consider the customs and traditions of the Philadelphia Mummers Parade without a sense of pessimism. Traditions have a way of hanging on, but this is not the case with the Parade. It has fallen victim to a kind of guerrilla warfare carried on by the City Fathers, the public at large, time, television, and neglect.

Over the years a great many traditions have built up around the Shooters and their Parade. Many of these have been handed down from father to son; many have developed without the knowledge of the paraders. Perhaps the most outstanding characteristic of the Parade in the early part of the twentieth century was the tradition that "the show must go on." There are numerous stories of men parading in near zero weather clad in nothing more than a loin cloth. The female impersonators seem to be the greatest sufferers from the weather, and the greatest heroes (heroines?) in ignoring it. In 1928, despite severe cold, seven female impersonators, attired in scanty evening gowns, were forced out of the Parade by a policeman, with the remark, "You can't flirt with pneumonia around here." The intrepid impersonators made a later attempt to sneak into the line of march, and finally had to be arrested for their own protection.

In 1929 the weatherman predicted a cloudburst. The majority of the marchers took his word for it, and stayed home; two Comic Clubs, however, insisted on marching. Several hours later, when the prediction came true, these nonbelievers were thoroughly drenched. The Parade was finally held on January 5, 1929. Another wet day, a fine drizzle kept up most of the time. Ticker tape and confetti drifting down from the office buildings in greeting to the Shooters stuck to their costumes, and created many strange colors, but the Parade went on.

In 1932 rain caused the Parade to be postponed to the following afternoon. By the time the Aqua String Band, which was the last club in the Parade, reached the finish line it was quite dark; spectators who desired to see this band had to turn on their automobile lights.

An article in *The Etude* of August 1947, gives another instance of this tradition:

> A Philadelphia string band on New Year's Day is surely a thing to see. The Mummers parade through storms and blizzards, with a heroism worthy of the "Charge of the Light Brigade." The picture shows the Polish American String Band, with gorgeous white shoulder pieces, marching through a baby blizzard on Broad Street, Philadelphia, last New Year's Day. It is reported that the string band players lost thousands of dollars in instruments, ruined on January first, this year.

Rain and snow are not the only enemies of the Mummers' long fight with the elements; fog has won more than one victory. One year the fog was so thick, old-timers claim, that the various clubs became confused and mixed in with their rivals to the great consternation of all. A gentleman on stilts fifteen feet high tripped over another Shooter and crashed to the ground; but, sticking to his stilts, he was up and above two minutes later.

For many years there was a movement on to have the Parade held at some time other than during the winter months, suggestions ranging from Halloween to the Fourth of July. In 1944, the Philadelphia *Evening Bulletin* held a poll on this matter; the question submitted to the people was: "Would the Mummers' Parade be more attractive to you if it were held another time of the year?" The answers were 51 percent "no," 35 percent "yes," and 14 percent "undecided."

In 1948 a spot-check of eighteen captains of clubs participating in the Parade, showed that all eighteen asked were in favor of keeping the Parade on New Year's Day. In this connection, however, Joseph A. Ferko, of the Ferko String Band felt at the time that it would be better to have the Parade sometime in the early spring or fall.

The Philadelphia *Evening Bulletin* published a report in 1948 from Mr. H. P. Adams, Senior Meteorologist, U.S. Department of Commerce, Weather Bureau, Philadelphia:

TWENTY-FOUR YEAR RECORD

Year	Weather	Temperature Range
1925	Clear	37-39
1926	Clear	27-40
1927	Clear	34-40
1928	Cloudy	30-27
1929	Rainy	39-46
1930	Occasional drizzle	42-44
1931	Clear and windy	33-31
1932	Heavy rain	41-44
1933	Clear	19-23
1934	Light rain	48-51
1935	Sleet and rain	37-36
1936	Partly cloudy, 5½ inches of snow on ground	26-31
1937	Clear	42-47
1938	Rainy	38-38
1939	Partly cloudy	42-46
1940	Clear and cold	17-20
1941	Clear	47-43
1942	Cloudy	35-39
1943	Cloudy	36-41
1944	Clear	38-39
1945	Heavy rain	53-56
1946	Cloudy and windy	29-32
1947	Snowy	31-29
1948	Rain, windy	36-33

There were only nine clear days during this period. Snow or rain occurred nine times. Temperatures were below freezing seven times and the only time the temperature was above 50 degrees a heavy rain fell.

A Suggestion: Why not a spring evening for the parade between May 28 and June 5? Decoration Day occurs between these two dates. Temperatures between 60 and 65 degrees could normally be expected which would be much better for the spectators. This period, from past records, shows the least chance of showers.

121

Strong reasoning to the contrary, tradition held sway. The Mummers have consented to parade in summer, fall, and spring, but they reserve the right to parade on their own day as well. However, with the great investment in costumes they were forced to forget the "show must go on" philosophy. Now, whenever the weather is threatening, the Parade is postponed; and so another tradition topples.

In the 1970 Parade the instructions of the Office of the City representative were:

> In case of inclement weather, marching decision will be made at 6:30 a.m. at Broad & Snyder, by the two directors of each division (Comic, Fancy, and String Band), Sam Karsevar, assistant parade director. Their decision will be telephoned to Room 204 and all media will be notified immediately. Postponement date will be Sunday, Jan. 4th.

When the decision is reached, the word is sent out that the Parade will or will not "go up the Street." This phrase has come to be part of the tradition of the Mummers, and is always used to relay the decision of the committee. The gentlemen confer, and if the decision is to start, they turn to the marchers and inform them that the Parade will "go up the Street." Broad Street is always referred to as "the Street" by the Mummers.

The Parade order is generally: Philadelphia Motor Police (alas Mounted Police are no more), Police and Firemen's Band, Parade Officials, Comic Clubs, Fancy Clubs, and String Bands. The route of the Parade over the years has varied. Generally it ran from Broad and Snyder—earlier the starting point had been Porter Street, five squares below Snyder (they are never blocks in Philadelphia)—to Girard Avenue, then east on Girard Avenue to Second Street, where it officially disbanded. Now it disbands at 6th and Arch, about nine squares from City Hall.

The order of march for the individual clubs is decided by drawing lots sometime before the Parade, usually late in November. The choice spots in the various sections are generally felt to be toward the end. The captains of the various clubs feel that the judges will remember the last clubs better than the first. As each unit is permitted only four minutes before the judges, this is sometimes an important consideration, and the captains are always glad to have first choice of position.

Each club requires a permit to parade, and this too has become one of the traditions that has fallen. In the past, these permits were granted on a first-come first-served basis. Billy Torelli, of the Comic Club of that name, made it a tradition to get that first permit. From 1940 to 1954 he received the first permit for parading, in most cases he came to City Hall the night before to get in line. Usually he waited seventeen hours for this privilege; then in 1954 the City decided to "modern up the thing" as Mr. Torelli put it, and began to issue blanket permits. So one more tradition has become a casualty.

One of the great traditions of the Parade of the past has been going down Second Street. When the Parade reached Second and Girard (remember that past tense) until fairly recently the marchers would go down Second Street. The South Philadelphia clubs, and some of the others, would have dinner, rest for a brief spell, and then start down Second Street. The local merchants donated money for additional prizes. This money usually ran around $800.00, but the Mummers would march for nothing. The entire population of the neighborhood would be out in full force; one-month-old babies, 100-year-old "youngsters" combined to give a rousing welcome to their own.

The residents of Second Street, below South, known as "two-streeters," long supplied the nucleus of the young and old men who participated in this great pageant, and coming down Second Street was the greatest thrill a Mummer could have. Here was the Parade as it must have been for over 150 years. The marchers were tired but relaxed; they were among their own, and acted accordingly. In the official Parade, the kissing of pretty girl spectators was forbidden: here it was encouraged, and the blackened cork, much in evidence, was daubed liberally on the girls.

By the time the Mummers reached Second Street it was almost dark, and the watchers had to strain to see them. Over the shuffling of feet could be heard the clear, bell-like tones of the glockenspiel, leading the String Bands in the "Golden Slipper." The Comic Clubs would take up the tune, and dance their Strut; waving their umbrellas to the rhythm of the dance. The spectators would join in the dance, and ond and young would cover the street.

The prizes had already been awarded in the "Uptown" Parade, and as the papers had not yet hit the streets, there was great interest on the part of the watchers as to who were the winners. There were no shrinking violets here; the victors proudly showed their true colors, and made no secret of their pride.

On one memorable day when Joe Ferko's String Band won first prize and he won the prize for best dressed captain, he marched down Second Street with a new broom, to indicate a clean sweep. As he proceeded block after block the news spread; Joe had won and was marching with a new broom held high. Second Street still remembers that night; it is one of the golden memories of this writer's childhood. Dusk, mist, grayish light, and Joe at the head of his band carrying a new broom held high to tell the world that his entry was the best in the Parade.

Alas, the custom of parading down Second Street is one more custom casualty. A few clubs still wander down the old path, but they get fewer each year. Interestingly enough, the casualty of another custom—the use of blackface makeup—helped temporarily reinstate the Second Street Parade. In 1964, when blackface makeup was banned, many of the clubs regrouped and once more went down Second Street with the cry "The Democrats own Broad Street, we own Second Street." Currently efforts are underway to revive this important part of the Parade.

This Parade is a family affair, father marching beside son. It is not uncommon to see three generations of one family doing the Strut on Broad Street. The Mummers are a warm, comradely group, and family ties are strong; this carries over into their Parade and is one of its chief attractions.

There are many famous Mummer families, and all have done their share in making Philadelphia famous for its Parade. The late George B. McClernand, Jr., former president of the Mummers' Association, started parading in 1913; his father and grandfathers, on both sides, were Mummers before him. The Durnings, father and son, paraded together for many years, and contributed much to the success of Philadelphia mummery.

For many years there were three generations of Tylers in the Parade every year; Harry, his son Joe, and his grandsons Joe, Jr., and Harry. Three generations of Wheelers—Hughy, Sammy, and Harry—annually donned the motley and marched up Broad Street.

The Rooney family, the Coyles, the Simmers, the Ables, and the Mooneys have been stalwarts of the Shooters. This "family" tradition is still going on; in 1970 the Quaker City String Band provided three generations of Bart Woods, father, son, and grandson.

The Mummers start young, and rarely give up their love of marching. One youngster, Howard C. Williams, Jr., paraded in 1939 with the Gallagher Club. He was only seventeen months old at the time, but behaved like the Mummer he was. His dad fixed him up with a high-chair with wheels, and kept him well fortified with milk. In 1947 he marched with the same club, and now at the ripe old age of thirty-four he entered his thirty-second Parade. His dad, Howard C. Williams, Sr., was President of the Mummers' Association in 1947.

From the official birth of the Parade, women have been forbidden to participate, and since that time they have been endeavoring to get into the act. They have tried many schemes and sometimes have succeeded in marching. There is a story told about a woman who, after making six costumes for men, dashed off one for herself, and entered the Parade. She won first prize, and never let her husband forget it.

In 1929, a woman reporter, Laura Lee, dressed as an Eskimo, worked herself into the Parade without being discovered. Billing herself as "Admiral Byrd's Girl Friend" she went the entire route undetected. She wrote a feature article in the next day's paper telling the Mummers all about it. Several years ago a young girl attempted to sneak into the line of march as a page-boy, but was "captured" before the Parade started. These are but a few instances; the Mummers have many stories of a like nature. During the war years, a mother of one of the Mummers who had entered the armed forces, paraded with a picture of her son, who was then serving overseas. She reached Broad and Race Streets, before the Parade officials caught up with her. Upon having the rules explained to her, she apologized and withdrew. In 1940, in honor of the Republican National Convention, the Mummers permitted a girls' band from Buffalo, New York, to parade with them. The following year they had to turn down great numbers of requests from all over the country.

Dogs might have been man's best friend for many years, but it was not until 1941 that they got the chance to prove their devotion via the Philadelphia Mummers Parade. Several Comic Clubs had the idea of working the dogs into the Parade. The trouble was not that the dogs loved men less, but that they disliked dogs more, and a pitched battle was soon struck up. Much of the morning was spent untangling wayward canines, and picking up upset Shooters. Dogs have not been popular since that time. In many of the great parades of Europe, and America, animals or representations of them are found, but not in the Philadelphia Mummers Parade. Animal representations are not popular unless that animal happens to be Donald Duck, a swan, or one of the three little pigs.

The average Mummer family holds open house on New Year's Eve and New Year's Day, and there is much friendly visiting. In the early days, the lady of the house would begin to prepare Philadelphia pepper pot from a recipe handed down from mother to daughter. Several large pots of this local soup were kept for visitors, as this would be the main meal for both days. The men of the house usually remained up all night celebrating the New Year and preparing for the big day. Quite often they would be out serenading most of the night. On New Year's Eve in South Philadelphia, String Band music and pepper pot were the mainstays. The custom of serving pepper pot on New Year's Day gave the wives of the Mummers time to get out and see the Parade. Today pepper pot is still served, and visiting continues, but on a much reduced scale.

There are many more traditions which have been carried on for generations but very few of the actual Mummers are even aware of them. The colors of the costumes are usually predominantly folk-colors: plush-red, bright yellow, and blue being the most popular. When asked why he uses these colors so often, the Mummer will reply that "bright colors stand up well in the sun." This is also the reason for the use of vari-colored sequins. This use of bright colors is one factor that is often forgotten by the spectators—this Parade is held in the bright of day, and the colors and costumes must hold their own in the sun.

The Mummers make great use of the sentimental flowers in their decorations. The daisy and the rose are by far the most popular flowers. Tulips are also used to a great extent.

Ostrich plumes are extremely popular, also, and play a great part in the history of the Parade. The cost of plumes often dictates the extent of the Mummers' decorations according to the *Sunday Bulletin*, December 25, 1966:

> "We designed our suits this year so we wouldn't have to use too many plumes," said Charles Molnar, captain of Palmyra String Band.

> "They are hard to come by," noted Henry Kunzig, Jr., president of Duffy String Band. "But we try not to reduce the number of plumes, because they're part of the color."

> Stoic James Young, 29-year-old captain of Oregon Fancy Club, added, "Let's face it, the increased price of plumes hurts, but you can always have another benefit to raise more money."

These plumes are purchased by the Mummers from two Philadelphia brothers, Sid and Sol Isserman, who get them from the South African town of Oudshoorn—according to the brothers the only source of these feathers. They are plucked from a herd of ostriches sixty-eight thousand in number.

One of the most interesting traditions of the Parade is the Strut. In the early days of mummery, when the various groups paraded individually, it was the custom to stop at local bakeries and private homes where the owners would give the Mummer captain a cake. These cakes would be saved for a grand cake-cutting party to be held sometime in January.

As the captain of the group would step forward to accept the cake, he would advance in a kind of strut. This is the step, somewhat more developed, that the Shooters use today when they dance to the "Golden Slippers." To give us a picture of these early days, here is a letter from Samuel Rodman quoted as written,

> Those shooters were rugged. Some did not sleep for 24 hours. After the parade they went from house to house getting cakes.

> The captain would make a little speech—some what as follows.

127

> Here we stand before your door
> As we did the year before
> Lay your pies on the table
> and we will eat they while we are able.

Music Sour

The band would hit some sour notes.

Lay your whisky on the shelf
We will come and help our self

Music Sweet

OH DEM GOLDEN SLIPPERS

The band would play The Bummers Reel, The Irish Wash Woman or Golden Slippers. Then the club would all get a drink and a cake. They put these cakes in a omibuss drawn by six horses all plunflds [?]. Some time in January they would have a cake cuttings. Sell tickets of $35c. hire a hall, put on a few half of beer and have a ball. You bought the beer for a nickle or 6 tickets for a quarter. This is how they made up the treasure.

Mr. Rodman was born in Philadelphia on June 14, 1896, and saw his first Parade in 1904 or 1905. Here are some of his recollections of the customs surrounding New Year's Eve and New Year's Day in Philadelphia at the turn of the nineteenth century:

One of the customs of the day was to carry a blond girl over the threshold of the door. I know because I was seeing a blond girl at the time, she was built like a truck. I could hardly lift her, but her mother made me do it. I did not marry her. I married one a little lighter. I have been married 50 year and very happy.

Some people had a dark complextion man come over the door. These supersitions were to keep jinks out.

My mother alway cooked sour krut and pork. The smell of the sour krut was to kill all bad omens in the house, to believe me the smell had to kill something. It was also the customs of some folks to have a sucking pig stuffed with chestnuts, oysters or krut and have a family gathering. We had one at our house many a time. You could go to one of the pig farms in the neck and get one dressed for about $2.00. The corner baker would roast it in his oven for 15¢.

Here is another one about the parade that you never hear tell of. "Vares big Mule." They had a big White mule about twice the size of a regular mule. They used him as a chain mule on the dumps on south Broad Street and at 4th & Ritner Street. For a few years this mule was always with the shooter parade. Don't let any one try to tell you this mule did not exist, because I got 5¢ from Vares stable boss to walk him in the stable yard, and water him and feed him on Saturday. I was just a kid. Vares stable was at 4th and Snyder Ave. Here is some thing else most people have

A String Band captain struts with his cape of plumes and hearts.

The selection of instruments is the source of the distinctive String Band sound. *Top:* The glockenspiel is a vital part of every band. Its bell-like melodies seem particularly striking in the bitter cold of New Year's Day. *Below:* Saxophones provide the volume and the melodies, while bass viols and banjos add rhythm.

Wearing the "trademark" of the Parade, the golden slippers, Mummers strut during their "Tribute to Ireland."

A Club turns the corner to City Hall with its "Tribute to Walt Disney."

Viewing a Fancy Club from above shows the circular costumes which weigh as much as eighty-five pounds.

The structure underneath a Fancy Club costume is rarely seen by a spectator. Notice the padding for the shoulders.

An all-star performance. The three-tiered umbrellas are part of the tradition of the Parade. The beginning of this particular feature is unknown.

A String Band drilling.

After the drill for the judges, a String Band marches off to await the award of prizes for which they have competed so fiercely and even, perhaps, to march down Second Street, as Bands have been doing for decades.

forgotten about. Between Thanksgiving and Christmas. There would be a club on the street most every night advertising the ball and trying out the band. Tickets for these balls were about 35¢. Then you went there and bought 6 tickets for 25¢ for beer, and you could dance. Most of these balls were held in a hall on the S.E. cor of 7th and Morris and in a hall on 2nd Street, north of McKean Street, but most of them ended in a fight. Some guy dancing with some one girl. The beer in those days was real german beer, not like the caned acid they are drinking to-day. I cant drink it so I stay on whisky.

There is one thing I would like to call your attention to. At no time did the bands ever play "Dem Golden Slippers" when the clubs were receiving a cake at the door. After the director made his little speech and called for music sweet the band always played The Bummers Reel, Hail, Hail the Gangs all here. Dem Golden Slippers was always used as a marching song. They always marched away playing Dem Golden Slippers. My mother gave many a cake to the B. E. Stevens club, and I followed many a club. These bands of to-day could not play the Bummers Reel "to fast." The two Camden Clubs were the toughest lot of men I know, they were not the best but they were tough. Just think what they did. They started out crossed the Kaighn Ave Ferry landed at South Street marched to Broad & Porter, went up the street to Broad & Girard ave. Then back to South Street Ferry then marched all over Camden. These shooters of to-day are soft. They were the Camden clowns and "the fire side of Camden." My hat goes off to them two clubs.

Triple-tiered umbrellas catch the eye on Broad Street on New Year's Day. As we have seen earlier, they are used by the marchers when they dance the Mummers' Strut. These umbrellas are swung to the rhythm of the music, the dancers bowing from the waist as they do so. This dance, called "the Strut" by Mummers, and "the Golden Slipper" by most outsiders, is always associated with the Parade, along with the term "Shooter." The question as to the difference between "Mummers" and "Shooters" often arises. The term "Mummers" is more popular with the general public than it is with the marchers themselves. Among the paraders, the term used is "Shooters," and invariably they go out New Year's Shooting. The only place the term "Mummers" is used consistently is in referring to the Mummers Parade. When they reorganized their association in 1940, the paraders changed the name from

Philadelphia Mummers' Association to the Philadelphia New Year Shooters' and Mummers' Association.

The peculiarly American characteristics of this Parade are better expressed in the term "Shooter" than "Mummer." "Shooter" carries the Parade back to its American origin and its "Neck" ancestry, and is unique with the Philadelphia Parade. The term "Mummer" was adopted by the public because it was the only term with which it was familiar, and because of the early English influence in the Parade.

However, the term "Mummer" is as much a part of tradition as is "Shooter," and many people today use the terms interchangeably, as I have in this book. No matter what we call them, the Shooter-Mummers still "dance and sing and prance and fling" on New Year's Day, now as they did of old.

Politics and politicians have been consistent in combating custom in the Parade. Whenever a large group of people combine to form some kind of organization, they become targets for political attention. As potential voting blocks, the Mummer organizations have been important to men seeking political power or political office. This attention has made itself felt in many ways and, in a sense, has become a part of the Mummer tradition.

The problem of politics, with respect to the Philadelphia Mummers Parade, falls into three categories. The first is concerned with the relationship between the City Hall leaders and the Mummers' Association. The second is concerned with politics within the various clubs. The third and the most important, in my opinion, is the custom of burlesqueing political figures and events.

The father of organized Philadelphia mummery is Bart McHugh, who as a public relations man carried great weight with Republican Mayor Ashbridge, who authorized the first official Parade. While he was the Parade director he ruled with an iron hand, permitting no one to interfere. There were no attempts on the part of City Council or the Mayor's office to exert any undue influence on the Parade during his tenure as director.

When Mr. McHugh died in 1932, George B. McClernand, Jr., was appointed director of the Parade, and served in that capacity until 1940. During that time there was an increase in the influence of City Hall on the Parade. The City Council appointed the judges and the directors of the Parade, and hence had a real bargaining unit in its control. This power was sometimes abused, and the Mummers felt that they should have more control over the Parade themselves. Mr. McClernand was the president of the Mummers' Association as well as the director of the Mummers Parade. In 1940 Director McClernand was notified by newly elected Councilman Joseph J. Milligan that he was to be replaced. Named as his successor was Councilman Milligan's 36th Ward Republican Lieutenant, John J. Shields. Mr. Shields, an old-time Shooter, was well qualified for the job, but the Mummers did not feel that Councilman Milligan had the right to change their leader without their permission. The consensus was that Mr. McClernand should be the only man to direct the Parade as long as the Mummers as a united body wanted him to do so.

Captain Harry Whitman, of the now-defunct Whitman String Band, said at the time: "We have been a political football long enough. Councilmen name the Parade judges, and hand out plums to their followers, while we parade and do all the work." Mummers all over the city protested, and a real fight was brewing. Mayor Samuels called in Mr. McClernand and told him that Councilman Milligan was a new man and had not known that a councilman cannot replace a former mayor's appointment. McClernand, who had been appointed by Mayor Lamberton, was told to sit tight. Satisfied, he left, and the big fight was over for the time being.

James Durning, a long-time Mummer, and the Mayor's chauffeur, suggested a compromise which stilled most of the muttering. He recommended that the job should be handled by both men. Mr. McClernand and Mr. Shields were to work together as directors of the Parade. This plan was accepted, and the Mummers settled down to work on plans for next year.

In November 1940, Councilman Milligan reminded Mr. McClernand that he would not be the director for that year's Parade. Again the Mummers held meetings and protested this action: feelings ran high. The decision as to who the Parade director was to be was still being debated when Mr. McClernand resigned his claim to that office. At that time he stated: "The Parade has moved up Broad Street for forty years with one director, and after that time it was decided to have two. There's no necessity for two of them."

Shortly after this Mr. McClernand resigned his position as president of the Mummers' Association to devote more time to his job in the Bureau of Internal Revenue. It was at this time that the Mummers' Association was reorganized. Councilman Milligan became chairman of the Committee on Celebrations.

The attitude on the part of City Council toward the Mummers Parade seems to be that of a fond parent to a wayward son. No effort is made to manipulate the Mummers' Association in rounding up votes nor, generally, to control the voting of its members. The effort seems to be aimed at keeping hold of the reins so that the Shooters will not get out of hand. So far it appears as if this attitude has been restrictive; the Parade has grown larger each year, but so have the number of restrictions imposed upon it. As the city appropriates the money for prizes and is responsible for the Parade, it seems sensible that it should exercise some form of control. If this control gets too oppressive, the City Council realizes that public pressure will be exerted. Therefore a balance of power is maintained, but it is slowly shifting to the city.

One battle the Mummers won out over the city was in the selection of judges for the Parade. The City Council, through its Committee on Celebrations, is responsible for the handling of the Parade and, as part of this duty, appoints the judges. For many years the Mummers maintained that these judges should not be appointed, but hired on the basis of experience and ability. There were many complaints about the decisions of the judges and, fair or not, the cry of politics was often raised by the losers. Mr. Joseph A. Ferko of the Ferko String Band stated that he felt that judges should be appointed for each phase of the Parade. He felt that there should be a judge for the music, another for the drilling, and a third for the costumes. In this way a fair decision could be reached, he maintained.

It took a political renaissance to break the hold of the City Council. In 1951, under a Democratic reform mayor and a strong new Council, the Mummers' Association was permitted to help in the appointing of judges. The selection was a particularly apt one, Ted Mack of the "Original Amateur Hour." Mr. Mack, assisted by his staff and Mrs. Ernest Truex, picked the 1951 winners. His selections met with general approval and, for the first time in years, the losers could not cry "politics." Prominent professional artists are used to judge the costumes, professional musicians are used to judge the music, and military men the drills. These men and women are not paid; however, they are presented with gifts each worth about $40.00. Their identity is kept secret so that they are free from pressure.

City politics do not play a very important part in individual clubs, in that policy is not dictated by political affiliations. In the early days when the City was predominantly Republican, the majority of the Mummers' clubs were Republican. It was estimated that eighteen of the twenty-seven clubs at that time were Republican.

Many of the leaders of the clubs in those days were active in politics. James Durning, of the Durning String Band, was Mayor Samuels' chauffeur for many years. Frank A. Costa, of the DeNero Comic Club was a member of the State Legislature, as was Joe Ferko. However, a majority of the Mummers' Association leaders do not make a living out of politics.

Occasionally during elections candidates hire String Bands to help win over the voters. This has led to accusations that certain clubs were dominated by politics. This was undoubtedly true in a few cases, but the average Mummer club is an independent group, beholden to no political party.

While the Shooters do not pay too much attention to city politics, they take their own association politics very seriously. In 1950, their presidential election almost erupted into the law courts. James Durning had been alternating in the presidency of the association, since its reorganization charter in 1940 forbade a president to succeed himself. He was president in 1942, 1944, 1946, 1948, and appeared to win the 1950 election, when he was challenged by John Mooney, Jr., of the Gallagher Club. In an election fraught with much bitterness and accusations of dictatorship, Mooney was elected by a fourteen to thirteen count. Durning demanded a recount, which was made. In the meantime, one of the delegates left and forgot to return, thus throwing the election into a thirteen to thirteen tie. Mr. Durning threatened to take the case to court, so a compromise candidate was suggested. This was John Hogg, a man who met the approval of both candidates. Mooney later became president of the Mummers' Association.

Another of the great early traditions of the Parade was putting the blast on politicians and politics. We have seen earlier that Councilman Charles O'Halloran put a stop to this in 1947, despite warnings from the Philadelphia *Evening Bulletin*. Mr. O'Halloran always seemed to have a short fuse when it came to Mummer fun. The Mummers love to poke fun at the foibles of mankind, and this sometimes gets on the nerves of the City Council. When the wage tax first went into effect, the Shooters really shot it down. In December 1942, Councilman O'Halloran put a stop to this satire. He said:

> Don't poke fun at the wage tax. After all, many city employees have received and merited and needed pay increases from the tax. It isn't a proper subject for caricature.

This attitude on the part of the city fathers brings up one of the most important functions of the Parade, that of safety valve. The Parade is a mirror of current social history and reflects all that is of importance to the public. It keeps the city leaders on the alert, for any mistakes they make will be held up to ridicule. When political leaders take it into their own hands and egos to censor too strictly this kind of satire, they are heading for trouble.

Don Marquis in his poem "The Gods at Coney Island" (*Noah an' Jonah an' Cap'n John Smith*, N.Y.: D. Appleton & Co., 1921) expresses it:

> Momus, the Jester of Olympus, dared
> To criticize the gods; Jove's anger flared
>
> In lightning, and he kicked the thing of mirth
> Forth from the outraged heavens, low as earth.
>
> The sequel hearken to, and ponder well:
> With humor gone, the great Olympians fell.
>
> Lacking the tonic whip, the stinging mind,
> The gods turned gross and presently declined.

Be that as it may, the city has managed to increase Parade restrictions since 1947. For example, mechanical or trick machines, such as the automibile which reared back, are now banned; no live animals are permitted in the Parade; and the canes or sticks with dice fixed to the ends carried by the clowns in the past are no longer allowed.

One cannot help but notice, in studying the Philadelphia Mummers Parade, that it is entering a new and lamentable phase. Spontaneity is losing out to regimentation. Thirty rules—twenty-nine written, one unwritten (the ban on political satire)—now regulate the Comic Division. In addition to these are thirty rules covering the Fancy Division, and twenty-nine covering the String Band Division. Each year these rules, which are mainly restrictive, increase, and the paraders lose still more of their sovereignty. Thus a once spontaneous, loosely organized, vital parade is becoming a highly organized, highly controlled, somewhat more sterile representation, and seems likely to remain so.

The most recent debilitation of the Parade has resulted from the intrusion of minority-group protest. Although organized Negro clubs do not participate in the modern Parade, one of the earliest clubs was founded by Negroes. Another group was assembled by Eph Horn who might have been a Negro (he was described as an "Ethiopian minstrel singer"). Horn brought out Beelzebub and Cooney Cracker, also the Prince of Egypt, who announced: 'Here I am the Prince of Egypt/ I am Pharaoh's only son."

Negro participation in the Parade is interesting. In 1906 the Golden Eagle Club, consisting solely of Negroes, put three hundred marchers in the Parade. At that time they claimed to have been founded forty years before, in 1866. The last Negro club to go out was the Octavius V. Cato, which last marched in 1929. Negro participation in the Parade is now almost non-existent.

Blackface makeup was used in the early days, the lampblack period, when marchers smeared their faces with lard and lampblack and went out visiting on New Year's Eve. As we know, the use of burnt cork or charcoal was one of the earliest methods by which man disguised himself and has no real relationship to American Negroes. In his *Folklore in the Old Testament* James G. Frazer reports many incidents of its use as a sign of mourning among the Indians of North America. The Romans used it in their Saturnalia. We have this speech by Cronus in Lucian's *Saturnalia*:

Mine is a limited monarchy, you see. To begin with, it only lasts a week; that over I am a private person, just a man in the street. Secondly, during my week the serious is barred; no business allowed. Drinking and being drunk, noise and games of dice, *appointing of kings and feasting of slaves,* singing naked, clapping of tremulous hands, an occasional ducking of corked faces in icy water—such are the functions over which I preside.

The use of burnt cork was a natural thing for a light-skinned person to use to disguise himself. The complement is found in the Trinidadian Carnival where the dark marchers threw flour on the dark spectators, much as the white marchers of Philadelphia rubbed burnt cork on the white spectators.

We find another comparison between Trinidad and Philadelphia—the "minstrel-hall Negro" is very much a part of the Carnival of Trinidad. This custom was probably brought to Trinidad by Trinidadians who had visited the United States. As Daniel J. Crowley puts it in his account of Carnival:

> The Trinidadian masquer, though nearly always a Negro himself, imitates these conventions including the "blackface," exaggerated white "lips" painted around his mouth, red spots on cheeks, and the "Uncle Sam" costume of scissor-tailored coat, tight striped trousers, white gloves, and tall beaver hat. He is thus a Negro imitating a white imitating a Negro.

The caricature of the Negro in America probably got its start with the singing and dancing of Thomas "Daddy" Rice in 1828. While appearing in Baltimore, Rice noticed an old, misshapen Negro slave, who continually muttered a silly ditty while performing strange contortions of his body. Rice introduced an imitation of this man into his own act. The greatest impetus to the minstrel-hall Negro imitation came with the publication of the anonymous "Jim Crow" in 1832. Forty-four verses long, it created for our times the stereotype Negro, and it is this caricature we have to contend with today. One need only look at the covers of "Jim Crow" and "Oh! Dem Golden Slippers" to be convinced of this.

All of this brings us up to the latest restrictions, the trial of a tradition, the banning of blackface makeup in the Philadelphia Mummers Parade.

The section of the city that still provides the majority of Mummers is the southern tier which, bounded on the north by South Street and on the south by the Delaware River, lies between the Schuylkill River on the west and the Delaware River on the east. This area is known as South Philadelphia. Here is its ethnic breakdown, all figures being taken from *Trends in Population Housing and Socio-Economic Characteristics* prepared under the direction of Alfred Toizer. The largest white ethnic group is Italian (62,129); the next largest is Russian, mainly Jewish (8,403); followed by Irish (4,346); and Polish (3,491). In addition there are 67,318 nonwhites, the massive majority of whom are Negroes. Most of the population of this section, both white and black, is between the ages of twenty and forty-four. The median for years of school completed by persons twenty-five years old and over is 8.3 for nonwhites, and 8.7 for whites. About 55 percent of the white males and 25 percent of the nonwhites are craftsmen, foremen, and operatives. There are 3,019 professional men among the whites, 196 among the nonwhites. An interesting sidelight is the listing of five farmers, all white, for this section.

About 60 percent of the houses in South Philadelphia are owner-occupied, and their median value is $5,802 for nonwhites, $6,992 for whites. The median rental is $57.00 for nonwhites, $62,00 for whites. The nonwhite median income in 1959 (the most recent census) was $3,677; for whites it was $5,624.

This is the locale of the beginning of the battle of the blackface.

It began on December 16, 1963, with the announcement of Elias Myers, Director of Parades, that blackface makeup for Mummers would be banned. Magistrate Myers' house was picketed. The result was a decision which pleased no one; blackface makeup would be allowed if it was to be used to create a character, but not if it was to be used to ridicule any ethnic group.

The Common Pleas Court of Philadelphia was asked by the National Association for the Advancement of Colored People to ban blackface makeup in the Parade. The organization's attorney, Charles Bowser, said:

> We feel that the city should not take part in a parade where Negroes are depicted in an unfavorable light, provoking, taunting, humiliating and embarrassing to them. We are taxpayers and we do not think our money should be used to support it.

137

In a letter to the Philadelphia *Evening Bulletin*, one Negro expressed himself to the contrary:

> As a Negro, I see no reason for feeling insulted because a few illiterate idiots in the community wish to smear their faces with

grease to cavort, clown and dance up Broad Street. Intelligent people are fully aware of the fact that the antics of this uncouth element of our society does not by any standard depict the true image of Negroes.

Both white and black resistance grew. Militant Negro groups claimed that they would stop the Parade with a chain made up of their bodies. Threats to "import" Negroes from New York and Washington to "operate" from rooftops were made. A brief respite was provided when the Parade was postponed because of inclement weather. The new date was set for Saturday, January 4, 1964. One of the warmest days in Mummer history (the temperature hovered around 40 for most of the day), saw one of the smallest crowds, and everywhere tension was felt. Three thousand policemen and policewomen were on duty to prevent trouble.

The white marchers paraded silently through the Negro districts in South Philadelphia. The majority of the bands refused to play, and all that could be heard was the sullen sound of muffled drums. A bus filled with policemen followed each unit; many were scanning the rooftops.

Few incidents were reported during the early stages. Then one of the Mummer clubs staged its own "sit-in." Members of the H. Philip Hammond Comic Club sat down in the middle of the street, some shouting, "Negroes sat down in City Hall, we'll sit down here." A new chant started: "One, two, three, four, we hate Cecil Moore" (local leader of the NAACP). The police quickly moved in and forced the Mummers to rise. The entire incident lasted about twenty minutes, after which the paraders again started up the Street.

As the Parade went around City Hall, some new, subtle elements of protest appeared. Here are notes taken from the Judges' position by the author:

PURUL: Dark blue makeup, green, white, a touch of black on one youngster. One clown rubbing on black grease paint as he goes before the judges—No reaction from the crowd. Two out of sixty have black streaks on their faces.

LIBERTY CLOWNS: Dark blue makeup, kinky hair.

LANDI: Red, white, blue face makeup. A showboat float, the musicians wear light tan makeup. Another float—a picture of a minstrel in blackface on a large poster with "Gone Yes— Forgotten Never." Al Jolson without blackface makeup.

HAMMOND: Real Negro on float—Blackface used by some Mummers—no reaction from the crowd. Young Negro boy dressed as an American Indian, elaborate costume, red makeup— shooting an arrow at a white youngster dressed as General Custer and carrying a sign "The Last of Custer's Last Stand."

As the Parade moved farther away from South Philadelphia, the police relaxed, the marchers moved rapidly, and the Parade regained some of its past joys, coming finally to a peaceful end.

The later unofficial but traditional march down Second Street was quiet, although the Mummers had the last word. As they got below South Street, the relative center of the Negro district, the blackface makeup reappeared. As darkness fell, the cry arose: 'The Democrats own Broad Street; we own Second Street." So, for the time being, ended the great blackface controversy.

A parallel situation erupted in New Orleans in 1961, when the Negro community boycotted the Mardi Gras because of the Zulu Parade. As this was an incident of Negro protest against Negro use of blackface, it might be of interest to explore.

The initial protest was signaled by an advertisement in the *Louisiana Weekly,* a Negro newspaper. In the form of a petition signed by almost twenty-seven thousand people, it read, as quoted by Calvin Trillin in *The New Yorker:*

> We, the Negroes of New Orleans, are in the midst of a fight for our rights and for a recognition of our human dignity which underlies these rights. Therefore, we resent and repudiate the Zulu Parade, in which Negroes are paid by white merchants to wander through the city drinking to excess, dressed as uncivilized savages and throwing cocoanuts like monkeys. This caricature does not represent us. Rather, it represents a warped picture against us. Therefore, we petition all citizens of New Orleans to boycott the Zulu Parade. If we want respect from others, we must first demand it of ourselves.

The Zulus voted to cancel their preparations, but were soon convinced by the mayor and the chief of police that they should parade.

The 1961 Mardi Gras Zulu Parade went on much as the 1964 Philadelphia Mummers Parade, with police protection for the

marchers. It was a hurried, almost somber procession, with two
members of the Police Department's canine corps protecting the
King's float. The 1962 and 1963 parades of the Zulus were little
better, and there was talk of cutting out the parade for 1964.
However, several weeks before Shrove Tuesday the permit to
parade was granted the Zulus.

In Philadelphia the Congress of Racial Equality threatened a
human barricade to stop the use of blackface; not so in New
Orleans. Oretha Castle, the president of the New Orleans Congress
of Racial Equality explained her stand.

> I think Zulu is a disgrace. . .we're split in so many different ways.
> We don't have just Negroes. We have our Catholic Negroes and
> our Protestant Negroes, our downtown Negroes and our uptown
> Negroes, our light Negroes, and our dark Negroes. And we have
> too many Negroes who don't think they're Negroes.

The Louisiana Weekly, which had criticized the Zulus in 1961,
covered the 1964 pre-Mardi Gras preparations as usual, casually
mentioning the Zulus.

Mardi Gras in 1964 went off with the Zulus leading with their
King Zulu in fine spirits, blessing his subjects as he rode by. The
day after Mardi Gras, upon being asked if the Zulu Parade might
indeed be ending because of the restrictions and the necessity for
police protection, the leader of the Zulus replied that he was sure
there would always be a Zulu Parade, and to date his prediction
has held true.

Perhaps the solution for the Philadelphia and New Orleans
dilemma lies in a fairly recent development in the Trinidad
Carnival described by Daniel J. Crowley:

> In more recent times the costume has been varied, one band of
> four minstrels appearing in suits, two black and two white, split
> down the middle and recombined so that each suit is half black
> and half white. The effect is completed by the hats, faces, shoes
> being black on one side and white on the other. A vaudeville
> routine of dance steps displayed this black-and-white effect.

Whatever the solution, the Philadelphia Mummers Parade and
the New Orleans Zulu Parade lie under a cloud of uncertainty not
likely to be dispersed in the near future.

In 1965 the Parade began to fight its blackface battle early. On November 13, 1965, Mayor Tate of Philadelphia announced that the blackface rule set forth in 1964 would be enforced.

> The policy is clear. It was adopted for the 1964 Parade and since then has been endorsed and fortified by the support of responsible individuals and organization, including the Commission on Human Relations and the Philadelphia Bar Association.

The Mayor's stand was endorsed by a member of the Archbishop's Commission on Human Relations for the Roman Catholic Archdiocese of Philadelphia:

> "It must go," said the Reverend John T. Mitchell. "To some it may sound like quibbling but when it's judged in relation to the whole picture it takes on a different light. Negroes associate it with something that runs deep in them: the dignity of the person and equality with other individuals."

Father Mitchell went on to say that perhaps the Mummers did not paint their faces black to make fun of the Negroes, but for the sake of racial harmony the practice should be stopped.

The Philadelphia Bar Association's Panel on Community Tensions requested that the city prohibit blackface makeup. To this request a former chairman of the Board of Governors, Laurence H. Eldredge, answered:

> The chairman of the Panel says that the underlying issue is "proper respect for the dignity of human person." It is nothing of the sort; the basic issue is whether the Mayor or City Council should be self-appointed censors of what people say and do, and whether they should prohibit conduct which some people don't like, and other people, with a sense of perspective and humor, find entertaining and amusing.

> If the Mayor and City Council can censor what the Mummers do (and it's one of the greatest shows in Philadelphia), why can't they censor what is said and done in our theaters? Why can't they prohibit books which contain detestable characters, who are protrayed as Negroes, or Jews, or Catholics, or Japanese, or whatever.

Theodore Voorhees, chancellor of the Philadelphia Bar Association was quick to answer Mr. Eldredge:

> ...the Mayor is only adhering to the views of the thoughtful members of the community who want to ban the blackface, not because there is anything morally wrong with it, but because in the context of today's racial problems, blackface has become for some a symbol of inferiority and buffoonery. . . .

> Mr. Eldredge and some of the paraders may think that blackface has no such effect, but the city sponsors the parade, puts up the prizes, maintains law and order and has the overall responsibility for the event. Mayor Tate's duty runs to all the citizenry, and in my opinion he is the one who should make the decision. I believe that his ruling is right and should be given the fullest support.

And so the battle went, its solution in the hands of the Mummers and the mayor. How it is to be ended depends on many factors, not the least of which is defining blackface makeup. In 1964 the marchers paraded in dark purplish blue makeup, and wore kinky hair; they were matched by others wearing dark brown, black striped, and black polka dot makeup. Could these justly be called blackface?

January 1, 1965, was brisk and windy, and the marchers moved rapidly. The shadow of the blackface controversy was still hanging over them as was indicated by the police supervision. Thirteen hundred police were assigned to keeping order, 410 in ten chartered busses which shuttled up and down the Parade route. This number was less than half the number assigned the previous year, and indicated a lessening tension.

At the start of the Parade the police ejected twenty-five Mummers for wearing blackface. However, fifteen were permitted to rejoin after they washed their faces. Four hardier or craftier clowns of the Hammond Comic Club made it to the judges' stand, and passed officially undetected. Hammond, the club which protested the most in 1964, complied with little protest in 1965. There were some interesting dark brown makeups combined with black pigtails, but these were in the minority.

One outcome of the controversy was the large number of unadorned faces, many only wearing rouge. This was particularly obvious in one brigade of the Landi Comic Club. Each clown was wearing makeup to match his costume: red costumes complemented by red makeup, etc. However, the black-costumed clowns wore no makeup at all. In another unit, where two Mummers depicted Ted Lewis and his famous "shadow," the shadow was without makeup.

In the 1965 Mummers Parade there was little resistance to the ban on blackface, and what there was came from the Comic Clubs with little to lose. Even on Second Street, the traditional home of the Mummers, this was evident.

By 1970 most marchers had accepted the restrictions with the same docility as they had all the others. The occasional lapse seems to be overlooked as are other violations of the regulations.

In conversations with them you are constantly told that the "Parade must go on," and you have the impression that they are running scared. The Mummers are afraid that the city will stop the Parade, and any concessions to avoid this have to be made. As for them, they are more concerned with conforming than conflict, parading than protesting. But as always with the Mummers there is the undercurrent, this undercurrent produced the only ballad yet written about the Mummers and their Parade:

THE BALLAD OF THE BLACKFACE CONTROVERSY
(To be sung to the tune of: Greenland Whale Fisheries)

T'was in nineteen hundred and sixty-four,
The day was January four,
The Mummers marched in their annual parade,
But not as they had before, big cowards,
Not as they had before.

There was a man named Cecil Moore
Who said, "No blackface worn,
Or you'll see the city of Philadelphia
Looked upon with scorn, big cowards,
Looked upon with scorn.

My people will scream and riot and yell,
An cause a great big fuss,
After all we've suffered at the white man's hands,
Why should they want to look like us, big cowards,
Why should they want to look like us.

143

OH DEM
GOLDEN
SLIPPERS

The city said now listen "Cecil,"
Your claim has got no ground
For years and years the Mummers have marched,
With their faces painted brown, big cowards,
With their faces painted brown.

But Cecil, he was not impressed
With the tradition of this function.
He went right up to that nice old judge,
And got a court injunction, big cowards,
Got a court injunction.

And now the big day is on hand,
The Mummer's faces are all white,
And we ask you, Cecil, what has this done,
To further the colored people's rights? Big cowards,
To further colored people's rights?

The above ballad was written January 4, 1964, by Bonnie Dinsmore, Linda McMichail, and Dolores Falcone.

And so we come to the end of one more tradition of the Philadelphia Mummers Parade. Like the other restrictions imposed upon this ancient and honorable tradition of a great city, this debilitation will be accepted philosophically by the Mummers. As one of them put it, "If that's what they want, that's what they'll get." And he joggled his triple umbrella, and strutted away up Broad Street.

LAUGHTER AND LIFE

And so we come to the end of our Parade, but the questions about it go marching on. What was its origin? What does it mean to the men who march? What does it mean to the city of Philadelphia? Why has it survived? These are the important questions concerning the Parade, and we will attempt to answer them.

Nothing is entirely black or entirely white when it comes to the Philadelphia Mummers Parade. How did it start? Think of it as a great river with many tributaries, and some turgid water from the slip-off slope. Or, think of it as a great snake, wriggling up Broad Street. Who created the tail, how important is the head? The tail for you, the head for me; neither works without the other.

First of all there were the Swedes. Dr. Francis B. Brandt's description we have already read. They disguised themselves as clowns, and went about the countryside shooting off guns. This is the head of the river, if you like. When the British arrived, they too practiced the customs of disguising and visiting over the New Year. We have seen that people were arrested for this practice. In 1702 John Smith was arrested for disguising himself as a woman and going from house to house the day after Christmas. However, the custom of disguising and visiting continued. The fact that the first arrest was for a switch in apparel is interesting and gives us some additional insight into the motivations of our early celebrants of the New Year; that is, the idea of exchange. Ernest Crawley has given this explanation of the practice:

The chief ideas in these ceremonial practices of exchange, whether of wives or other possessions, are, primarily, the wish for a preliminary interval before starting a new life, a sort of *vitai pausa* or artificial gulf between the old and the new, while there is implicit in the exchange an act of disguise; and secondarily, a

145

desire for union with one's fellows, which is actually effected by exchange of identity....Hospitality is a close form of union. Exchange of wives, of dress, of names, of positions, or of anything belonging to a man, alike produces union. This secondary result of the common practice of men and women dressing up in the garments of the other sex, . . .is that the two sexes are united, just as they are united in theory and in practice in the so-called licence used on such occasions.

This probably was the basic motivation originally; however, the British settlers actually did not believe in the theory of exchange. Custom lingers long after belief ends. So they were following habits from their homeland, where they had a long history of disguising. One aspect of this cultural background was the English Lord of Misrule, and the Scot's Abbot of Unreason. These were leaders in a kind of Saturnalia. Here is a formal permission written by Richard Evelyn, Esq. for the Lord of Misrule outlining and appointing one Owen Flood to be Lord of Misrule over Evelyn's estate at Wooten, Surrey:

> *Imprimis,* I give free leave to Owen Flood, my trumpeter, gentleman, to be Lord of Misrule of all good orders during the Twelve days. And also, I give free leave to the said Owen Flood to command all and every person or persons whatsoever, as well servants as others, to be at his command whenever he shall sound his trumpet or music, and to do him good service, as though I were present myself, at their perils.

> I give full power and authority to his lordship to break up all locks, bolts, bars, doors and latches, and to fling up all doors out of hinges, to comebat those who presume to disobey his lordship's commands.

The twelve days referred to were those between Christmas and Epiphany. During these days great merriment and fun-poking prevailed. In Scotland these days were called the Daft Days. The merrymaking took place in churches, colleges, and cities of all sizes. This is another contributor to our Parade, as the English practiced the custom of playing the fool.

Add to this the practice of performing the English Mummers' Play, and you have one more drop of water. This play depicts a mock battle, death, and recall from death, and is given usually over the Christmas holidays. Most scholars feel it is part of an ancient fertility rite aimed at renewing life after the long winter. E. K. Chambers in his *The Mediaeval Stage* states that it might have been given originally in the spring, and been drawn to Christmas by the Christian Church leaders. This play was given in the United States frequently, Breck in his *Recollections of Samuel Breck with Passages from his Note-Books,* reporting it in Boston in the middle of the eighteenth century, and Scharf and Wescott in their *History of Philadelphia* in Philadelphia in the early nineteenth century. From this practice in Philadelphia probably came the idea of costuming over the holidays, other than the switching of clothing between men and women. An article in the *Journal of American Folk-Lore* in reporting a Christmas play in St. Louis at the turn of the century gives us some idea of what those costumes might have been like.

> The costumes of the players were very crude, intended merely to suggest the characters. Old Father Christmas wore a fur cap and fur gloves, a long red coat, and top boots. He had a wig and beard of long white hair, and the end of his nose was reddened. Beelzebub wore a large black hat, called a dripping pan, and a long black coat. The Valiant Soldier wore a blue soldier's suit and soldier's cap. Little Dick Nipp wore a hat on the end of which a pig's bladder was tied. He was the "fool" or fun-maker of the play. St. George wore a small hat with a feather in it, a dark red coat, knee-breeches, and low shoes, and carried a sword.
>
> The play was in two parts. After the performance, the players were usually rewarded with hot spiced ale or cider and bread and cheese, and in addition to this a sum of from two to five shillings was collected.

Besides the description of costumes, the above account gives us one more clue to the tradition in Philadelphia—the collecting of dole in the form of liquid refreshment, food, and money. What appears to have happened in Philadelphia is that the play was forgotten but the custom of visiting and collecting from neighbors continued. The people of Philadelphia took over what Chambers calls the "debris of ritual custom" and made it into their own ritual, retaining only the presentation speech. As they visited from door to door using this speech, they added some forms of music and entertainment, usually crude. The earliest account of this activity is found in Christopher Marshall's *Diary* in 1782.

This was the beginning of our Parade. From this the evolution-ary process took over, held back somewhat by the Parade's period of illegality from 1808 to 1859. This might be termed the river's underground period, for we know that it kept on flowing and growing under the surface.

The real flood tide came after the Civil War. The United States took a deep breath; the twentieth century moved in. So did a lot of people from other countries. The Irish and Germans followed pretty much the pattern already set by the British settlers. The Germans called their celebrations "Bellsnicklin," and readily blended into the mainstream. The Irish too blended into the flow, but added their own pageantic impulse which found its expression in the procession. In Ireland there was a long tradition of processions in honor of the saints of the Church. There were processions for St. Brigit, St. Patrick, St. Peter, St. Martin, St. Stephen, and St. Bartholomew. But the festival above all others, the one that overshadowed all was that celebrating All-Hallows Eve. With the Irish, this holy day had a strong feeling of family reunion. It was felt that the souls of the dead would return to their families for this night. Doors were left opened for the easy access of ancestors, dishes of food were left out, and tobacco was made available. And there was a procession:

> In Co. Cork there survived well into the last century a Hallowe'en ceremony similar to the well-known Mari Lwyd of South Wales: a procession was led by a figure clad in a white shirt and carrying a horse's head. This "white mare" was followed by youths blowing cowhorns, and as they stopped to levy toll from farmhouses they recited a long string of verses savouring strongly of paganism. Hallowe'en bonfires and noisy demonstrations remind us that these features of Guy Fawkes' Day have, in England, been stolen from the older festival.

With this kind of background, the Irish immigrants found themselves right at home in Philadelphia's pageant, and it is after their arrival in fairly large numbers that the greatest impetus to the growth of the Fancy Divisions came. To this day the Fancy Divisions have a great many members of Irish extraction. In my opinion, it was no coincidence that the suggestion for all the marchers to join in one grand procession came from an Irishman, Bart McHugh.

The Italians, somewhat later to immigrate in large numbers, moved into the Parade later. However, they brought a new element—Carnival. The early Parade had been somewhat stiff, even though rowdy. With the advent of the Italians came the flaming color of the Saturnalia—after all, their ancestors invented it. The Latin temperament tinted the cold colors of the Anglo-Saxons and the Celts, and the Comic Clubs resulted. The Italians did not invent the Comic Clubs, but they created the atmosphere that made their development inevitable. The Italians are still the strongest ethnic group in number in the Comic Clubs.

To this procession-parade-pageant-carnival the American Negro James Bland contributed his music, the theme song of today's marchers, "Oh, Dem Golden Slippers," and made it the Philadelphia Mummers Parade: a composite of English, Scotch, Irish, Swedish, Italian, Negro, and American culture.

Now, what does this Parade mean to the men who march? The cardinal sin of megalopolis is that it integrates cities and states, but disintegrates societies and social units. The people of Detroit had integrated housing in 1967, but had to riot to impress the power structure that equal housing was not enough, that they needed recognition as human beings as well. What has this to do with the Shooters? Plenty! The Parade gives them a stake in the community that is uniquely their own. Every man must have his club, a place to belong, and a reason for existence. Most people cannot express this need, but they feel it. The Mummers' clubs help people meet this need by providing fellowship, expression, and recognition.

Each year the Mummers are talked about and written about more than the previous year. Invitations are received by the dozens requesting their presence at special events. Even London has succumbed to Mummer magic:

> Next Wednesday afternoon London is going to get a taste of Philadelphia when Miss Liberty Belle, Lida Welycko, is hostess at a party in the new Villager boutique 183 Sloane St. in Knightsbridge during her brief trip to England.
>
> Besides making Londoners more aware of Villager fashions, that are made in Philadelphia and sold in a boutique that is a replica of Villager and Ladybug shops in our city and suburbs, she will join some of her fellow Philadelphians in striving to change London from a swinging town to a strutting town.

149

The strut is, of course, the famous Mummers Strut that will be performed by Philadelphians now living in London. They will don suits of satins and plumes and dance in the streets around the Villager Shop. The costumes, by the way, are being provided by the Mummers' String Band Association.

All this points to the general appreciation the community feels for the Parade and its Shooters. This community feeling works both ways: it gives the Mummers their sense of belonging, and gives the community a feeling of ownership.

This brings us to the most important contribution the Parade makes to the men who march, a feeling of community consciousness and service, and the answer to the question posed at the head of this chapter. It permits them to participate in a warm, friendly, and human way in unifying their city for one day at least. Where they failed during the 1964 Parade in their controversy over blackface makeup, they only reflected the failure of society in general, and should not be held as separately guilty. Generally, the Shooters give Philadelphia a common denominator of laughter and life that is almost as old as man. At each year's beginning, the town is taken over by a community project, representing the efforts of people from every section. Young and old inquire about the Parade and make plans to see it. Parents get up early in the morning in order to ensure their children a good place along the route of march. The city is filled with music, life, and color from daybreak until long after dusk. One million people gather together with a common desire—entertainment. No one can pass through Philadelphia on this day without catching the spirit and the meaning of this Parade, and what it means to the men who participate.

The history of the Philadelphia Mummers Parade has been one of growth. Starting in a section of South Philadelphia known as "the Neck," it has gradually spread through the city and surrounding countryside. As the city has grown, the Parade has grown. Its history has not all been serene; nevertheless, it has progressed, has developed a character and a distinctive personality of its own. It is raucous, yet dignified; satirical, yet sentimental; but above all, it is friendly. To watch it from the sidelines is to become part of it. This special quality of warm friendliness is one of its major characteristics, and one that makes it stand out from almost all other parades. There is no feeling of aloofness when the Bands begin to play on Broad Street. Thus the first gift the Parade brings to Philadelphia is an atmosphere of friendliness and fun to start the year off right. What are some of the other contributions?

The Parade is more or less a local phenomenon, and it is felt by some that the business it brings to the city is mostly local. This is not the case, however, for thousands of visitors come here especially to see this spectacle. They patronize the shops, stay in local hotels, and eat in local restaurants. The railroad companies advertise the event, and run special trains to Philadelphia from towns in New Jersey, New York, and Delaware, as well as towns in Pennsylvania. This brings business to the city, and profit to its residents.

The restaurants that do the most business during the march period are the less expensive, quick-service type, such as Horn and Hardart's. Many of the small luncheonettes also do a rushing business. Street vendors and small merchants who remain open during the day usually make out very well. In general, the business picture is very good for the service industries.

Business over New Year's Eve is normally good, and it is felt by many that the Parade does not increase it in any sizeable amount. There is one important point to keep in mind in this respect—the Parade does keep people in the city all day. Many visitors wait to see the Shooters, and thus bring an extra day's business to local agencies, which adds to the holiday period profits.

An important factor to keep in mind when considering the financial picture of the Parade is the amount of business it brings to local costumers and piece-goods manufacturers. The Mummers spend many thousands of dollars on material alone, and many more on hiring craftsmen. Carpenters are hired to build the floats, tailors to make the costumes, and buildings are rented in which to work. Many professional costumers assist the Mummers in their work.

The 1947 Parade cost the Mummers' Association at least two and a half times more money than it did in 1946. James Durning, president of the Association at the time, said in this connection: "Due to the rise of prices our association is spending $100,000 for costumes this year, and we, the Mummers, feel the prize

151

money should be raised above the present proposal." This $100,000 is a real contribution to local coffers, where most of it went, and at today's prices is undoubtedly twice that now.

The bars and hotels of the city do excellent business over New Year's Day, but it is felt by some businessmen that the Parade does not increase this business. Their argument is that people are in a convivial mood over New Year's Eve anyway, and would entertain and be entertained regardless of the Parade. This is not altogether true, however. Undoubtedly people do come to Philadelphia expressly to see the Parade—the many special trains and busses coming into the city on New Year's Day offer evidence of this fact. Others who are in the city for New Year's Eve stay over to witness the Parade on New Year's Day. These people must sleep somewhere, and it seems logical that some must stay in midtown hotels, thus bringing them some extra business. The bars along the route of march share in this extra business during the Parade period. Thus is appears that the bars and hotels of the city do enjoy increases because of the Shooters. Most of them deny this fact because they are afraid they might be asked to contribute to the prize money.

The law-enforcement situation during the Parade is mostly concerned with the direction of traffic, and, as the Parade grows in size, this problem increases. This is a serious item of expense to the city. Usually, most available city policemen are on duty for that day. An example of this problem was given when the Mummers were asked to march during the Franklin Celebration in 1937. Airplanes were used to direct traffic. Flying back and forth across the line of march, the pilot kept in constant two-way radio communication with radio-equipped police cars below, informing them of traffic snarls. That day there were 2,000 city police and 200 park guards on duty. In 1964, 3,000 policemen and policewomen were required to control the march. In 1970 the number of on-duty policemen was not as great; however, there was a sizable number.

With the $76,500 the city currently donates in prizes, the cost of extra police protection, and possible property damage, the city budget increased by at least $250,000 because of the Mummers Parade. This is the estimate of a member of the city administration. Even if we divide this estimate by half, and come up with $125,000, it is still a sizable sum. Does the city profit from its investment? A categorical answer to a question involving so many intangibles as this would be impossible. However, it appears that the city does profit from this Parade.

The national publicity alone would be worth $125,000, or $250,000, and the Parade is nationally important because of television. Here is a comment from the *Los Angeles Times* of Thursday, November 23, 1967, concerning Thanksgiving day celebrations; but it does bring publicity to Philadelphia:

THOSE SWINGING MUMMERS

Of course you don't have to watch football. A lot of Americans get up early to turn on the Thanksgiving Day parade which, in color particularly, is a delight for the Kiddies. For those who like catchy music there's nothing like the Mummers' Parade in Philadelphia with those string bands bringing back the old marching favorites and reminding listeners that the banjo, strummed enthusiastically, is the dancingest musical instrument there is.

And then from the other coast, comes this announcement in *Yankee Magazine* of September 1967.

In MASSACHUSETTS the biggest of them all, the Eastern States Exposition, is held on the Exposition Grounds in West Springfield, this year from the 16th to the 24th. The Exposition is a prime example of the breadth and scope of today's fairs, only more so, and this month is making yet another addition to its full-scale program by adding star performers to be featured in free coliseum shows. Head-lined will be the Supremes, hailed as the leading female vocal group in the country; and throughout the nine-day run of the Exposition there will be a Mummers Band from Philadelphia, a Gay 90s exhibit, Victor Borge with his "Comedy of Music," comedians Allen and Rossi, who will have with them Shari Lewis and others.

The Parade is known not only in the United States, but in Europe as well. James Bone, a Scot, at the time London editor of the *Manchester Guardian*, said of it:

153

It was the most perplexing sight I have seen in America. There were in it hints of all sorts of American origins; in the red Indian motif of the feathered headgear, bands around the brow and tassled tunic, but all these were transfigured and colored as Bakst might have rhapsodized them. . . .

I have seen shows in many countries, but this was unique in the appropriate scale of its decorative effects for a street masquerade, in the handsomeness of the young men Mummers, the spirit within the frolic that made it a work of art, particularly in the dancing and the rather solemn mien necessitated and appropriate to the high head gear and the elaborate wigs of the masquers.

This type of publicity is of inestimable value to the merchants of the city. Each time the name of Philadelphia is mentioned at home and abroad the citizens of the city profit. Philadelphia is an industrial city as well as a city of homes, and its industries need all the contracts and contacts they can get.

This Parade is economically productive in that it brings over $200,000 dollars to artisans of the city; and more thousands of dollars to the local merchants. Philadelphia has become known as the Convention City, and part of the credit for this reputation must go to the Mummers, as they have always been one of the city's major attractions, and their Parade has always been a feature of the larger conventions. The total cost to the city is about $250,000 according to estimate. For this it receives national and international publicity, and large sums of money in added revenue. Thus it appears that its investment brings it a substantial profit.

Be that as it may, we are now to our final question. Why did this Parade survive in Philadelphia? First of all there is the spirit of the Mummers themselves as shown in this letter by Joe Farrell in the *Evening Bulletin*:

> I like the Mummers' Parade and I like the comic division and as one string band club captain said, the parade and your own division gets in your blood and when it does you stand up for what you believe in. The comic division brings joy and laughter into the hearts of many people New Year's Day and when I hear or read of someone putting it down, I want to fight.

Add to this the geography of the city, and the way it was laid out by William Penn. The great, long, straight Broad Street deserves some credit for the Parade's longevity. It makes it possible to frame the production adequately, and allows easy access to it by the spectators. Then, too, the size and character of the city help. It has kept the personality of a small town. The

154

massive cities of the country have not been able to maintain a personal parade. St. Louis, New Orleans, Pasadena, and Philadelphia have successfully maintained parades because they have remained relatively small towns psychologically. New York City and Los Angeles have been unsuccessful in maintaining parades of this nature because they have become too spread out and too impersonal.

Luck, too, had its contribution to our Parade's long life. Bart McHugh and the twentieth century found just the right time to begin to consolidate 150 years of pageantry. Time and place coincided to make the city proud of the Parade, and the paraders proud of the city.

This, then, is the history of a Parade in the city of Philadelphia; a monument to its greatness and its tolerance. This is one more side of the city founded by the Quakers and dedicated to Brotherly Love.

Much of the information about the early part of this century has come from unpublished recollections, the Clubs themselves, and personal conversations with individual Mummers. Among those who provided information were John Baukus, Louis N. Callazzo, Joseph A. Ferko, Albert Fink, John Gilbert, Harry Hodgson, John Mooney, Sr., David Nelson, Bernard Samuels, and Billy Torelli.

Written materials, often vaguely dated, but as old as forty years or more, were as follows: letters from William Brennan, David W. Crawford, J. S. Herbert, J. Wesley Myers, Samuel Rodman, and Fred A. Winkler. There were other materials from Jack Hines, C. B. Tustin, Sr., and Christopher Marshall.

The Frank A. Collins NYA, Kensington String Band NYA, Lobster NYA, Wildwood String Band, and the Joseph A. Ferko String Band had invaluable information.

I have also depended upon the annual *Mummers Magazine,* the *Evening Bulletin* and *Sunday Bulletin,* the *Inquirer,* the *Evening Public Ledger,* the *North American and United States Gazette,* the *General Aurora Advertiser,* and *Poulsen's American Daily Advertiser* (all of Philadelphia) and the Easton, Pennsylvania, *Sentinel.*

Additional bibliographic information, as well as a fuller treatment of the historic and folkloric aspects of the Mummers' Parade, is on file in the University of Pennsylvania Library under the title "A History of the Philadelphia Mummers' Parade."

BOOKS

Alford, Violet. *Introduction to English Folklore.* London: G. Bell and Sons, Ltd., 1952.

———, and Gallop, Rodney. *The Traditional Dance.* London: Methuen and Company, Ltd., 1935.

Banks, M. Macleod. *British Calendar Customs, Orkney and Shetland Islands.* London: Published for the Folk-lore Society: William Glaisher, Ltd., 1946.

Baring-Gould, William A., and Baring-Gould, Cecil. *The Annotated Mother Goose.* New York: Charles N. Potter, Inc., 1962.

Biddle, Henry D., ed. *Extracts from the Journal of Elizabeth Drinker, 1759-1807.* Philadelphia: J. B. Lippincott Company, 1889.

Bourboulis, Photeine. *Ancient Festivals of "Saturnalia" Type.* Periodic Publications of the Society of Macedonian Studies, Supplement 16: Thessaloniki, Hellenika, 1964.

Bridenbaugh, Carl. *Cities in the Wilderness.* New York: Harper Brothers, 1952.

Chambers, Edmund K. *The English Folk-Play.* New York: Haskell House, 1966.

————. *The Mediaeval Stage.* London: Oxford University Press, 1963.

Chambers R., ed. *The Book of Days: A Miscellany of Popular Antiquities,* 2 vols. Detroit: Republished by Gale Research Company, 1967.

Collections of the Historical Society of Pennsylvania. Philadelphia: Historical Society of Pennsylvania, 1853.

Crawley, Ernest. *The Mystic Rose.* London: Spring Books, 1965.

Dorson, Richard M. *Buying the Wind: Regional Folklore in the United States.* Chicago: University of Chicago Press, 1962.

Dulles, Foster Rhea. *The United States Since 1865.* Ann Arbor: The University of Michigan Press, 1959.

Eberhard, Wolfram. *Chinese Festivals.* New York: Schuman, 1952.

Evans, E. Estyn. *Irish Folk Ways.* New York: Devin-Adair Company, 1958.

Frazer, James George. *The Golden Bough,* 1 vol. abr. ed. New York: The Macmillan Company, 1948.

————. *Folklore in the Old Testament,* 1 vol. abr. ed. New York: Tudor Company, 1923.

Gallop, Rodney. *Portugal: A Book of Folk-Ways.* Cambridge, England: The University Press, 1936.

Gaster, Theodor. *New Year: Its History, Customs and Superstitions.* New York: Abelard-Schuman, 1955.

Gilbert, Daniel R. "Patterns of Organization and Membership in Colonial Philadelphia Club Life, 1725-1755": unpublished Ph.D. Dissertation, University of Pennsylvania, 1952.

Gregor, Walter. *The Folk-Lore of the North-East of Scotland.* London: Elliot Stock Company, 1881.

Grimm, Jacob. *Teutonic Mythology,* trans. James Steven Stallybrass, from the 4th ed., 4 vols. New York: The Dover Company, 1966.

Hazlitt, W. Carew. *Faiths and Folklore of the British Isles,* 2 vols. New York: Benjamin Blom, 1968.

Henderson, William. *Notes on the Folk-Lore of the Northern Counties of England and the Borders.* London: W. Satchell, Peyton, and Company, 1879.

Hori, Ichire. "Mysterious Visitors from the Harvest to the New Year," *Studies in Japanese Folklore,* ed. Dorson, Richard M., adv. eds. Mabuchi, Toichi, and Oto, Tokihiko. Bloomington: University of Indiana Press, 1963.

James, E. O. *Seasonal Feasts and Festivals.* New York: Barnes and Noble Inc., 1961.

Lichen, Tun, translated by Bodde, Derk. *Annual Customs and Festivals in Peking,* 2nd ed. Hong Kong: Hong Kong University Press, 1965.

Marquis, Don. *Noah An' Jonah An' Cap'n John Smith.* New York: D. Appleton and Company, 1921.

McNeill, F. Marian. *The Silver Bough,* 3 vols. Glasgow: William MacLellan, 1961.

Myers, Albert Cook, ed. *Narratives of Early Pennsylvania, West New Jersey and Delaware.* New York: Scribners Company, 1912.

Oberholtzer, Ellis Paxson. *Philadelphia, A History of the City and Its People,* 4 vols. Philadelphia: S. J. Clarke Company, n.d.

Powell, J. H. *Bring Out Your Dead.* Philadelphia: University of Pennsylvania Press, 1949.

Scharf, J. Thomas, and Wescott, Thompson. *History of Philadelphia,* 3 vols. Philadelphia: L. H. Everts, 1884.

Scudder, H. E. ed. *Recollections of Samuel Breck with Passages from His Notebooks.* Philadelphia: Porter and Coates Company, 1877.

Shakleton, Robert. *The Book of Philadelphia.* Philadelphia: The Penn Publishing Company, 1918.

Sprogle, Howard O. *The Philadelphia Police, Past and Present.* Philadelphia: Privately Printed, 1887.

Tallant, Robert. *Mardi Gras.* New York: Doubleday Company, 1948.

Tiddy, Reginald J. E. *The Mummers' Play.* Oxford: The Clarendon Press, 1923.

Weiser, Francis X. *The Holyday Book.* New York: Harcourt, Brace and Company, 1956.

Withington, Robert. *English Pageantry: An Historical Outline,* 2 vols. New York: Benjamin Blom, 1963.

Wright, A. R. *British Calendar Customs: Movable Feasts.* London: Published for the Folk-Lore Society by William Glaisher, Ltd., 1936.

_____.*British Calendar Customs: Fixed Festivals, January to May Inclusive.* London: Published for the Folk-Lore Society by William Glaisher, Ltd., 1938.

_____. *British Calendar Customs: Fixed Festivals, June to December Inclusive.* London: Published for the Folk-Lore Society by William Glaisher, Ltd., 1940.

Toizer, Alfred, compiler: *Trends in Population Housing and Socio-Economic Characteristics.* Philadelphia Planning Analysis Sections, City of Philadelphia Community Renewal Program, November, 1963.

PERIODICALS

Burne, Charlotte S. "Guisers' Play, Songs and Rhymes, from Staffordshire," *The Folk-Lore Journal,* 4:350 (Jan.), 1886.

Crowley, Daniel J. "The Traditional Masques of Carnival," *Caribbean Quarterly,* Double Issue, v. 4. nos. 3 & 4, March 1956, June, 1956.

Egan, Maurice F. "A Day in the Ma'sh," *Scribner's Monthly,* 22:350, 1881.

"Fiddling in a Blizzard," *The Etude,* 65, no. 8, 1941.

Frey, Julie. "On Pepper Pot," *Greater Philadelphia Magazine,* 42:10, 1954.

Hall, Marjory. "A Fair Month," *Yankee Magazine,* 31, no. 9:31, 1967.

Potamkin, Harry. "Mummers of Quaker City," *Theatre Guild Magazine,* n.v., January: 41, 1930.

Simpson, Sarah H. J. "The Federal Procession in the City of New York," *The New-York Historical Society Quarterly Bulletin,* 9:39, 1925.

Taylor, Antoinette. "An English Christmas Play," *Journal of American Folklore,* 22:389, 1909.

Trillin, Calvin. "The Zulus," *The New Yorker,* 40, no. 25:42, 1964.

Udal, J. S. "Christmas Mummers in Dorchester," *The Folk-Lore Record,* 3:87, 1880.

APPENDIX

1970

Comic Division

RULES AND REGULATIONS

The following suggestions and information are provided in order to assist you in accurately, fairly, and quickly determining the prize winners of the various competing units with the Comic Division.

It is suggested that 50 points be used as the maximum by judges in determining awards to participants.

1. Each Comic Club shall:
    a. Have a banner in front of the Club designating the name of the Club.
    b. Keep an interval of one city block.
    c. Have at least one hundred (100) costumed marchers.
    d. Have at least one brass band consisting of a minimum of fifteen (15) playing musicians with brass instruments only.
    e. Furnish a brass band to play at or near the judges stand while parade participants perform.
    f. Designate a Captain to represent the Club for the day of the parade.

2. A sound system must be a component part of a Float, Brigade, Group, etc., and not a substitute for a brass band.

3. The following are not permitted under any circumstances:
   a. Sticks or canes.
   b. Animals.
   c. Fireworks.
   d. Commercial advertising or commercialism in any form.
   e. Smearing spectators with make-up or any form of improper conduct.
   f. Intoxicating beverages.
   g. Blackface.

4. Automobiles are permitted only when decorated and carrying a sign designating a theme for a contestant. Each Club shall be permitted one emergency car.

5. The following shall be the prize categories:
   a. *Club Prize*—This prize is awarded to the Club having won the most prize awards. But, for example, if one Club is awarded thirty prizes and another twenty-eight, the latter could be declared the winner, depending if it excels in outstanding originality, beauty, and workmanship. But, if one Club should receive thirty and the other nineteen, then it is apparent that the Club winning the thirty prizes should be awarded the first prize.
   b. *Captain's Prize*—Awarded to a costumed individual designated as Club Captain. The costume can be on wheels but not motorized. The Captain cannot use the assistance of page boys.
   c. *Brigade Prize*—Awarded to twelve (12) or more fully costumed individuals depicting a central theme designated by a title sign.
   d. *Float Prize*—Awarded to any object on wheels, fully decorated and designated by a sign, setting forth the title. Individuals on the float must be fully costumed commensurate with the theme depicted.
   e. *Group Prize*—Awarded to not less than three (3) nor more than eleven (11) individuals in full costume depicting a central theme designated by a title sign.
   f. *Most Original Character Prize*—Awarded to an individual for a portrayal of a person of history, stage, music, science, fiction, notoriety, etc.
   g. *Most Original Costume Prize*—Awarded to a fully costumed individual on the basis of construction and novelty of costume and/or originality and uniqueness of idea.
   h. *Funniest Couple Prize*—Awarded to two individuals who together depict a central idea or theme which is original and unique, and/or whose costumes are novel, neat, and colorful.
   i. *Juvenile Prize*—Awarded to anyone under twelve (12) years of age on the basis of costume and theme.
   j. *Special Mention Prize*—Awarded at the discretion of the judges to any of the contestants who deserve to win a prize but who have not been awarded a prize under any of the designated categories.

Awards 1 to 7—Brigade, Group, Floats

Awards 8 to 15—Original Character, Original Costume, Funniest Couple, and Juvenile.

6. Each Club and Club Captain shall be awarded a prize. However, all other designated prize categories shall total fifteen (15) prizes for each category. Cards are to be handed to judges at the judging stand by one man representing each Club. Cards should designate the name of the Club, the category, the theme, and the name of the person wearing the costume. No prizes will be awarded unless card is presented to the judges.

1970 COMIC PRIZE LIST
Prize Money Total — $19,100

MOST ORIGINAL CHARACTER

CLUB			GROUP	
Prize	Amount	Prize	Amount	Prize	Amount
1	$2550	1	$75	1	$125
2	2500	2	70	2	110
3	2450	3	55	3	95
4	2350	4	45	4	80
5	2200	5	40	5	70
		6	35	6	60
		7	30	7	50
CAPTAIN		8	30	8	45
		9	30	9	45
Prize	Amount	10	30	10	40
1	$200	11	25	11	35
2	175	12	20	12	30
3	150	13	20	13	30
4	125	14	20	14	25
5	100	15	20	15	25

MOST ORIGINAL COSTUME

BRIGADE				SPECIAL MENTION	
Prize	Amount	Prize	Amount	Prize	Amount
1	$200	1	$75	1	$100
2	185	2	70	2	95
3	170	3	55	3	85
4	150	4	45	4	75
5	130	5	40	5	65
6	115	6	35	6	55
7	100	7	30	7	50
8	90	8	30	8	45
9	80	9	30	9	40
10	70	10	30	10	35
11	60	11	25	11	30
12	55	12	20	12	25
13	50	13	20	13	25
14	50	14	20	14	25
15	50	15	20	15	20

FUNNIEST COUPLE

OH DEM GOLDEN SLIPPERS	FLOATS			FUNNIEST COUPLE			JUVENILE	
	Prize	Amount		Prize	Amount		Prize	Amount
	1	$150		1	$75		1	$50
	2	145		2	70		2	40
	3	135		3	55		3	35
	4	110		4	45		4	30
	5	90		5	40		5	25
	6	80		6	35		6	25
	7	70		7	30		7	25
	8	65		8	30		8	15
	9	60		9	30		9	15
	10	55		10	30		10	15
	11	50		11	25		11	15
	12	45		12	20		12	15
	13	45		13	20		13	15
	14	45		14	20		14	15
	15	45		15	20		15	15

1970

Fancy Division

RULES AND REGULATIONS

1. All Clubs must have a Captain suit or float with one representative and a maximum of 10 men or page boys (Total 11).

2. All Clubs must have at least one entry in each category and have at least one band or music of not less than fifteen (15) playing men. Female Impersonator to be optional.

3. Floats will be allowed in the parade for Club Captains and Brigades only, but they must not be of a commercial nature.

4. No animals, livestock, fowl, mammals, reptiles, or fish will be allowed.

5. The only automobiles to be permitted in each Club's line of march are as follows: One auto in front of club (Banner Auto); one motor vehicle for each Brigade and Fancy Club Captain's Float. One car at the end of the parading Club. Any infraction of this rule will cause a deduction of 100 points from the club total.

6. Club prizes will be awarded by the point system. (Points to be set up by the parading Fancy Clubs.) Each individual prize (to be determined by the judges) would receive so many points. The Club with the highest number of points will receive First Prize, etc.

162

7. All costumes must start and finish the official route of the parade to qualify for prizes.

8. One designated man to each judges stand from each Club to hand in cards, pre-collected, before reaching each judges stand. The cards must specify what category the costume is in.

9. The Juvenile classification must consist of one suit, carried by only one child and not included in any other groups or classification. The age limits for juveniles must range from 12 years or under.

10. Trio Pantomime Clowns must state on their cards "Trio Pantomime Clown" or they will be disqualified. No drop curtains allowed on these suits.

11. Any suit in line, except Juvenile or Female Impersonator, may compete for Handsome Costume Prize but to consist of only one suit to be carried by only one man around the Hall.

12. All King Jockey, King Clown, and Handsome Trim suits must be a frame suit consisting of a yoke and spreaders (six-foot minimum spreaders) and legs. Also, wheels are optional. If wheels are used they must stay on the suit; they cannot be taken off.

13. Trio Clown and Trio Jockey to be open-faced suits, e.g., individual undergarment to be visible from front. Minimum dimensions for headpeice 9' wide and 6' high above shoulders. Plumes and points included in measurements. Directors are to enforce size.

14. Jockey Trio's undergarment to represent Jockey and Clown Trio to represent Clowns. No old Brigade or Special Mention suits to be used for Trio Clown and Trio Jockey suits. Trio Clown to have drop curtains on back.

15. Special Mention category will cover any entry in the Fancy Division excepting any Brigade, and frame suits consisting of a yoke and spreaders and legs. All entries must have 19 participants or less, 20 or more will constitute a Brigade.

16. Costumed or uniformed bands are not to be judged for prizes. They will only supply the music for the line of march. No band is allowed to perform at judges stand.

17. All Brigades must have at least twenty men in costume to compete for and be eligible for prizes. In the event of postponement due to inclement weather, seventeen men will be acceptable on the postponed parade date.

18. Brigades will be permitted to use musical and imitation musical instruments excluding those which are used in a String Band other than drums. Instruments such as bongo drums, marrocas, tambourines, gongs, cymbals, bells (not glockenspeil), whistles, and so forth are permissible.

19. Brigades will be judged on the point system. The points being 70% for beauty of costume and 30% for presentation of theme.

20. All Brigades must have new suits to be judged and awarded prizes. Directors will inspect costumes.

21. Any protest or infraction of the above rules must be submitted to the Fancy Directors, who will forward said protest to the judges for their ruling on whether a costume in question is an infraction of the rules, on the day of the parade. Both Directors will have disqualification cards and make final decisions. Also, the President of the Fancy Division to be

granted permission to assist Directors and have same facilities available as Directors on New Year's Day.

22. Each Club will appoint one man to form a committee at City Hall to help point out infractions of the rules to judges and to go over the prize winning cards before the judges make them final. (Stress)

23. No String Band costume will be allowed to enter in the Fancy Division.

24. No one in the Special Mention Category will drill at the judges stand.

25. Two-thirds (2/3) of the members of a Brigade must be 18 years of age or older to qualify as a Brigade.

26. Brigades will be permitted 30 seconds get ready time at first yellow line, each Brigade will be limited to 4 minutes drill time in drill area. The time will start at end of 30 seconds or when the first line of march across first yellow line, whichever comes first. Time will stop when first line of march crosses second yellow line. One point will be deducted by each judge from presentation points for an infraction of this rule. Any Brigade drilling over 4 minutes and 30 seconds from the starting time will be disqualified.

27. Prizes will be awarded to 4 best dressed Brigade Captains.

28. Blackface will not be permitted in the parade.

29. All groups, brigades, and individuals must be committed to one of the Fancy Clubs before New Year's Day. No groups, brigades, or individuals will be accepted on the day of the parade.

30. There are now twenty-three (23) Brigades committed and permitted to parade. However, in the future if any of this number (23) drops out, a maximum of twenty (20) Brigades will be allowed, with a maximum of five (5) Brigades for each Fancy Club.

1970 FANCY PRIZE LIST

Prize Money Total — $23,050
Total Points — 2,398

	CLUB		TRIO CLOWN			PANTOMIME CLOWN	
Prize	Amount	Prize	Amount	Points	Prize	Amount	Points
1	$2350	1	$275	50	1	$115	7
2	2050	2	250	40	2	105	5
3	1800	3	225	35	3	95	3
4	1600	4	170	30	4	65	2

CAPTAIN

Prize	Amount	Points
1	$700	100
2	600	85
3	500	70
4	400	55

HANDSOME TRIM

Prize	Amount	Points
1	$250	50
2	225	40
3	200	35
4	175	30
5	150	25
6	125	20

JUVENILES

Prize	Amount	Points
1	$85	10
2	75	9
3	65	8
4	55	7
5	45	6
6	35	5
7	30	4
8	25	3
9	25	2
10	25	1

BRIGADES

Prize	Amount	Points
1	$500	70
2	475	65
3	450	60
4	400	55
5	370	50
6	330	45
7	290	40
8	230	35
9	200	30
10	175	25

KING JOCKEY

Prize	Amount	Points
1	$240	50
2	215	40
3	190	35
4	165	30
5	145	25
6	120	20

FEMALE IMPERSONATOR

Prize	Amount	Points
1	$60	6
2	50	5
3	40	4
4	30	3
5	20	2
6	10	1

HANDSOME COSTUME

Prize	Amount	Points
1	$325	60
2	300	55
3	275	50
4	250	45
5	225	40
6	200	35

KING CLOWN

Prize	Amount	Points
1	$240	50
2	215	40
3	190	35
4	165	30
5	145	25
6	120	20

SPECIAL MENTION

Prize	Amount	Points
1	$260	55
2	240	50
3	225	45
4	215	40
5	190	35
6	165	30
7	135	25
8	115	20
9	95	15
10	80	10

TRIO JOCKEY

Prize	Amount	Points
1	$275	50
2	250	40
3	225	35
4	170	30

BRIGADE CAPTAIN

Prize	Amount
1	$70
2	40
3	30
4	25

String Band Division

RULES AND REGULATIONS

Rules and Regulations for the 1970 New Year's Parade which are to be applicable to all contestants who compete in this division for prizes.

1. All String Bands must have at least 48 players in the line of march and not more than 10 non-playing costumed members at any point of the compass, either vertical of horizontal (including aides). Each Band may have a maximum of 64 playing men plus 1 playing musical director. If the parade is postponed because of bad weather each Band must have at least 45 playing men on the day the parade is held.

2. No floats of any type or kind shall be allowed in the String Band Division.

3. No brass or cup instruments, such as trombones, French horns, etc. are permitted.

4. The following point system shall be followed for the judging of the String Bands: 40 points for music; 40 points for costume; and 20 points for presentation.

5. Each Band shall be allowed four minutes in front of judges.

6. The judging area will be identified by the painting of white lines showing the starting and finishing points or a stationary white flag at starting point and stationary checkered flag at finishing point. This judging area shall not contain any obstructions such as TV trucks, etc.

7. No Band shall countermarch or go to the rear on Juniper Street before the white starting line, and no Band shall countermarch or go to the rear on Juniper Street after they leave the judging area except to go north on Broad Street.

8. The Time for judging each Band shall officially begin when the first line of musicians crosses the starting line and the official time for judging shall end when the first line of musicians crosses the finishing line; or after four minutes within judging area whichever is the earliest.

9. A timekeeper will be assigned to time each String Band.

10. Each Captain must carry his own garment without assistance from any other person.

11. Signs, insignias, or decorations of any kind carried on the front of cars are to be no higher than 50 inches from street level and no larger than 6 feet in length.

12. Clubs may carry banners. Only the name of the Band can be on the banner. No elaborations, no trimmings.

13. An authorized man or men will be stationed at Broad and Porter streets to measure all signs and decorations and the Captain will be informed

immediately of infraction of Rule 11. The Captain can make the necessary changes before starting.

14. Each String Band shall be allowed two pleasure cars in its line of march, one in front and one in rear of Band. Each Band shall stay within a distance equal to a city block.

15. Any type of amplification either on instruments or connected in any manner whatever with String Bands is absolutely prohibited.

16. No animals of any kind are permitted in the String Band Division.

17. No females are permitted to march. Any infraction of this rule will result in immediate disqualification.

18. Any String Band violating the above rules and regulations is automatically disqualified to last prize. If there are two bands disqualified then the first band that was disqualified moves up to the next prize.

> Example: 1st Band Disqualified — 18th prize
> 2nd Band Disqualified — 19th prize
> 3rd Band Disqualified — 20th prize

19. Any String Band marching in old suit or costumes renovated shall be ineligible for any prize except last prize.

20. No name professional performer is allowed to parade with a String Band. Passed at meeting, September 13, 1956.

21. Any band reporting late New Year's Day morning at Broad and Porter streets shall go to the end of the Philadelphia Bands. This means their designated time. Passed at meeting, November 12, 1959. Judges should be notified of such changes in parade positions.

22. A Band may be permitted to play from the South side of City Hall to the starting line. However, NO drilling will be permitted. A thirty (30)-second preparation period at the starting line will be allowed each band. Once a band starts to play music they must continue their forward motion into the judging area.

23. There shall be no electrical illumination used in adorning, or as a part of any String Band costume.

24. No String Bands will be allowed to use blackface in parade.

25. No canes, no smoke bombs or fire crackers allowed.

26. No special instruments of any order shall be used in parade route.

27. A Band must have at least forty (40) playing members in new costumes to parade, otherwise they will not be allowed to enter the line of march. A Band must have at least forty-eight (48) playing members in new costumes to compete for prizes.

28. One truck will be permitted to advertise the current String Band "Tribute Album" and the Convention Hall "Show of Shows."

29. No literature or programs to be used by the judges in judging the String Bands except cards presented by the aides.

1970 STRING BAND DIVISION PRIZE MONEY
Prize Money Total — $34,350

OH DEM
GOLDEN
SLIPPERS

Prize	Amount
1	$2,470
2	2,370
3	2,270
4	2,170
5	2,070
6	1,970
7	1,870
8	1,770
9	1,670
10	1,570
11	1,520
12	1,470
13	1,420
14	1,370
15	1,320
16	1,270
17	1,170
18	1,120
19	1,020
20	870
21	725
22	550
Total	$34,025

Captain's Prizes

1	$ 125
2	100
3	75
4	25
Total	$325

STRING BANDS

Winners	Prize Money	Theme
1915		
1.		
2.		
3. Fralinger		
1916		
1. Talbot	$150	
2. Victoria	50	
3. Fralinger	50	
1917		
1. Talbot	150	
2. Fralinger	100	
3. Oakey	50	

168

Winners	Prize Money	Theme

1918

1. Talbot — 150
2. Trilby — 100

1919

No Parade

1920

1. Fralinger — 350
2. Aronomink — 250
3. Trilby — 150

1921

1. Quaker City — 350 — Bulgarians
2. Fralinger — 250 — Neapolitan Minstrels
3. Hegeman — 150 — Hawaiians
4. Aqua — Mexicans

1922

1. Quaker City — 350 — Hindu Prince
2. Hegeman — 250 — Minstrels of Charles 2nd
3, North Philadelphia — 150 — Cossacks
4. Aqua — 100
5. Trixie

1923

1. Aqua — 350 — Kewpie Dolls
2. Ferko — 250 — Rudolph Valentino
3. Hegeman — 150
4. Quaker City
5. Trixie
6. North Philadelphia
7. South Philadelphia
8. Beach Progressive Club

1924

1. Hegeman — 500
2. Aqua — 400 — Prince Charles
3. Ferko
4. Quaker City
5. Trixie
6. North Philadelphia
7. Wildwood
8. Steubing
9. Franklin

1925

1. Hegeman — 1,000
2. Ferko — 750 — Mah Jong
3. Trixie — 600
4. Wildwood — 500
5. Aqua — 400
6. Kensington — 350
7. Steubing — 300
8. North Philadelphia — 250
9. Dixie Serenaders — 150

1926

1. Hegeman — 1,000 — Captain Kidd and the Pirate Band
2. Ferko — 800 — Sesqui-Centennial Serenaders
3. Wildwood — 650

Winners	Prize Money	Theme

4. Aqua
5. Steubing
6. Kensington
7. Trixie
8. Lawndale

1927

Winners	Prize Money	Theme
1. Ferko	1,100	Cards
2. Wildwood	900	Cohorts of Caesar
3. Steubing	800	
4. Hegeman	700	
5. Kensington	600	
6. Trixie	450	
7. Woodland	300	Oriental Clowns

1928

Winners	Prize Money	Theme
1. Hegeman	1,000	Harem Girls
2. Wildwood	900	Ming Dynasty
3. Ferko	800	Musical Aces
4. Steubing		
5. Kensington		
6. Woodland		
7. Trixie		
8. O. V. Cato		Fancy Clowns

1929

Winners	Prize Money	Theme
1. Ferko	1,200	Stars
2. Wildwood	1,100	
3. Hegeman		
4. Kensington		
5. Woodland		
6. Trixie		American Doughboys
7. O. V. Cato		

1930

Winners	Prize Money	Theme
1. Ferko	1,600	Guards
2. Hegeman	1,300	
3. Wildwood	1,200	
4. Kensington		
5. Aqua		
6. Woodland		
7. Trixie		Breakway (?)

1931

Winners	Prize Money	Theme
1. Ferko	1,550	French Fans
2. Wildwood	1,250	
3. Woodland	1,150	Aztec Indians
4. Kensington		
5. Trixie		
6. 69th Street		
7. Aqua		
8. Broomall		

1932

Winners	Prize Money	Theme
1. Ferko	750	Fantastic Indians
2. Woodland	600	Peacocks
3. 69th Street	500	
4. Aqua	400	
5. Trixie	250	
6. Kensington	250	
7. Quaker City	150	

Winners	Prize Money	Theme

Non-Prize Winners
Broomall
Philadelphia

1933

Broad Street Parade	*No Prizes*	
Aqua	(1st)	
Broomall		
Ferko		A Victory Revue
Golden Slipper	(2nd)	
Hegeman		
Philadelphia		
Trixie		

Stadium Parade	*No Prizes*	
Kensington		
Quaker City		
Woodland	(3rd)	American Indian
69th Street		

1934

No Broad Street Parade. Each Band paraded in its own neighborhood.

1935

1. Quaker City	650	Fans
2. 69th Street	500	
3. Ferko	450	March of the Harlequins
4. Hegeman		
5. Aqua		
6. Polish American		
7. J. J. Morrow		
8. Broomall		
9. Kensington		
10, Woodland		Prince of Music
11. McCracken		

1936

1. Ferko	700	Maharaja of India
2. Polish American	600	Old Glory
3. 69th Street	500	The Top Hatters
4. Hegeman-Lancaster	400	
5. Quaker City	300	
6. Trilby	200	
7. Milton Rose	150	
8. Woodland	100	Musical Artists
9. Aqua	25	
10. Broomall	25	
11. South Philadelphia	25	
12. Connors	25	Musical Troubadors
13. J. J. Morrow	25	
14. Dickson	25	
15. Kensington	25	
16. Rogers	25	

1937

1. Ferko	800	The Northern Lights
2. Woodland	600	The Spider and the Fly
3. 48th Ward	500	American Jockies
4. Quaker City	400	
5. Aqua	350	

OH DEM GOLDEN SLIPPERS

Winners	Prize Money	Theme
6. Broomall	300	The March of Time
7. Polish American	250	Musical Follies
8. J. J. Morrow	225	
9. Trilby	200	
10. Greenwood	175	Vikings
11. Hegeman	150	
12. Milton Rose	125	
13. Myers	25	
14. Dickson	25	

Captain's Prizes

Winners	Prize Money	Theme
1. Joseph A. Ferko	25	Ferko String Band
2. Raymond Endriss	15	Quaker City String Band
3. James Durning	10	48th Ward Strong Band

1938

Winners	Prize Money	Theme
1. Ferko	1,200	The Heralds of Peace
2. Aqua	1,000	Ali Baba
3. Quaker City	900	The Kings Harlequins
4. 69th Street	800	
5. J. J. Morrow	700	Marching Fountains
6. Myers	600	Sunrise
7. Trilby	500	Revolutionary Era
8. Hegeman	400	The Roman General Troupe
9. Broomall	250	Jack Frost and His Snow Crystals
10, Polish American	200	Holland Dutch Boys
11. 48th Ward	50	Holland Dutch Boys (?)
12. Young Starts	50	The Three Musketeers
13. Woodland	50	Dutch Boys
14. Greenwood	50	Men From Mars
15. Dixon	50	Oriental Scenes
16. Milton Rose	50	College Colors
17. Uptown	50	Star Dust
18, Belmont	50	Kewpie Dolls

Captain's Prizes

Winners	Prize Money	Theme
1. Elmer W. Leyrer	50	Aqua String Band
2. Joseph A. Ferko	30	Ferko String Band
3. Robert Rodenbough	20	J. J. Morrow String Band

1939

Winners	Prize Money	Theme
1. Ferko	1,200	Day and Night
2. Polish American	1,000	Stars and Stripes
3. Feltonville	900	Hopi Indian God
4. Aqua	800	The Lost Valley of Asia
5. Quaker City	700	
6. 48th Ward	600	American Indians
7. Broomall	500	The King of Swing
8. Woodland	400	Prince Kador
9. 12th Ward	300	Prince Charming
10. Uptown	200	Mexicali Rose
11. Young Stars	100	Be My Valentine
12. Myers	100	
13. Hegeman	100	Flower Garden
14. Greenwood	100	Robin Hood
15. Trilby	100	
16. 69th Street	100	Mountain Hill Billies
17. Dixon	100	Alexander's Rag Time Band

Winners	Prize Money	Theme
Captain's Prizes		
1. Elmer W. Leyrer	50	Aqua String Band
2. Joseph A. Ferko	30	Ferko String Band
3. Alfred E. Fink	20	Hegeman String Band

1940

Winners	Prize Money	Theme
1. Quaker City	1,200	The Prince of India
2. Polish American	1,000	Over the Rainbow
3. Ferko	900	Lohengrin
4. 12th Ward	800	Deep Purple
5. Young Stars	700	Old Glory
6. Woodland	600	Dove of Peace
7. Feltonville	500	Proud Peacocks
8. Myers	400	American Eagles
9. Whitman	300	Scarlet O'Hara
10. 48th Ward	200	The Harp That Once Through Tara's Hall
11. Broomall	100	Gainsborough's Blue Boy
12. Hegeman	100	Argentines
13. Uptown	100	East Comes West
14. Trilby	100	American Clowns
15. Aqua	100	Wings of America
16. Greenwood	100	South American Gauchos
17. South Jersey	100	All American Bartenders
Captain's Prizes		
1. Harry Tyler, Jr.	50	Myers String Band
2. Joseph A. Ferko	30	Ferko String Band
3. Raymond Endriss	20	Quaker String Band

1941

Winners	Prize Money	Theme
1. Polish American	1,200	All the World Is Waiting for the Sunrise
2. 48th Ward	1,100	The City of Philadelphia Flag
3. Feltonville	1,000	Royal Turkish Guards
4. Whitman	900	The King's Jesters
5. Ferko	800	Boys of the Golden West
6. 38th Ward	700	Devil in Flame
7. Bell	575	Melody Ranch
8. 26th Ward	475	Musical Senoritas
9. Broomall	375	Yankee Doodle Boy
10. Hegeman	275	Fans of Melody

Non-Prize Winners

Winners		Theme
Aqua		New Orleans Mardi Gras
Fralinger		The Spirit of 1776—Minute Men of 1941
Greenwood		Stars and Stripes
Myers		A Tribute to the Boy Scouts of America
Quaker City		The Land of the Midnight Sun
Uptown		Rapsody in Blue
Woodland		Head Hunters
Young Stars		Russian Cossacks
12th Ward		Fountain of Melodies
35th Ward		Symphony in Black and White

	Winners	Prize Money	Theme
	Captain's Prizes		
OH DEM	1. Harry Whitman	50	Whitman String Band
GOLDEN	2. James Durning	30	48th Ward String Band
SLIPPERS	3. Harry Tyler, Jr.	25	Myers String Band
	4. Charles Boettinger	15	Young Stars String Band
	5. Joseph A. Ferko	10	Ferko String Band
1942			
	1. Bell	1,300	American Indians
	2. Ferko	1,200	The Parade of Jewels
	3. Quaker City	1,100	King Tut-en-Kamen
	4. Myers	1,000	
	5. 48th Ward	800	Beauty in Our American Skies
	6. 35th Ward	750	Tyrolean Holiday
	7. Fralinger	600	Stars of Victory on Parade
	8. Polish American	500	Moonlight and Roses
	9. 38th Ward	400	Any Bonds Today
	10. Uptown	300	V for Victory
	11. Aqua	225	Mr. Freedom Man
	12. Whitman	200	Kick Conga
	13. Woodland	150	Modern Crusaders of 1942
	14. 12th Ward	100	Moon Over Miami
	15. Greenwood	100	Devil Dogs of America
	Captain's Prizes		
	1. James Durning	75	48th Ward String Band
	2. Raymond Endriss	50	Quaker City String Band
	3. Alfred E. Fink	40	Myers String Band
	4. Charles Bremser	10	38th Ward String Band
1943			
	1. Hegeman	1,600	A Prayer for Victory
	2. Bill Morrows	1,500	The Bells of St. Mary's
	3. Polish American	1,300	When the Lights Go on Again
	4. Quaker City	1,100	Men of Shangri-La
	5. Fralingers	1,000	Is Everybody Happy
	6. Ferko	950	The Crusaders of Freedom
	7. Woodland	900	Say It with Music
	8. Uptown	700	Glorified Rose
	9. 12th Ward	500	Liberty
	10. Whitman	500	The Road to Morocco
	11. Aqua	450	Yankee Doodle Dandies
	12. Broomall	400	The Spirit of Chang-Kai-Chek
	13. 38th Ward	300	
	14. 25th Ward	250	Cadets of 1943
	15. 5th Ward	200	
	Captain's Prizes		
	1. James Durning	100	Bill Morrow's String Band
	2. Raymond Endriss	50	Quaker City String Band
	3. Edward Piskadlo	25	Polish American String Band
1944			
	1. Quaker City	700	
	2. Ferko	600	Red Cross Crusaders
	3. Aqua	550	
	4. Polish American	500	
	5. Fralinger	400	Dixieland Minstrels

Winners	Prize Money	Theme

6. Durning	350	
7. 35th Ward	300	
8. Uptown	250	
9. Hegeman	225	
10. Woodland	200	
11. Broomall	175	
12. Avalon	170	
13. 5th Ward	165	

Captain's Prizes

1. James Durning	50	Durning String Band
2. Alfred E. Fink	25	Hegeman String Band
3. Raymond Endriss	10	Quaker City String Band

1945

1. Quaker City	850	Polar Prince
2. Durning	750	Old Glory
3. Ferko	700	Garrison Warriors of the Far East
4. Polish American	650	Our Colors
5. Woodland	550	How Many Hearts Have You Broken
6. Hegeman	450	Honoring the Gold Stars
7. Broomall	400	Oriental Fantasy
8. Fralinger	300	Alexander's Rag Time Band
9. Aqua	250	Skeiks from Bagdad
10. Avalon	225	Gentlemen of Swing
11. Uptown	200	The League of Nations

Captain's Prizes

1. James Durning	35	Durning String Band
2. Joseph A. Ferko	25.	Ferko String Band
3. Raymond Endriss	15.	Quaker City String Band

1946

1. Durning	720	Stars of America
2. Quaker City	620	Musical Cadets
3. Polish American	570	Till the End of Time
4. Ferko	520	Rays of the Rainbow
5. Hegeman	420	A Bit of Old Moscow
6. Aqua	300	Carnival of Silver Bells and Laces
7. Woodland	250	Russian Cossacks on Parade
8. Fralinger	150	Penn's Treaty
9. Avalon	100	Holiday in Mexico
10. Broomall	100	The Atomic Age
11. Uptown	100	Musical Clowns
12. Fire-Fighters	100	Far East Warriors

Captain's Prizes

1. Raymond Endriss	25	Quaker City String Band
2. James Durning	15	Durning String Band
3. Walter Krop	10	Polish American String Band

1947

1. Ferko	1,400	25th Anniversary Bouquet
2. Quaker City	1,300	Legion of Peace
3. Durning	1,200	MacNamara's Band
4. Aqua	1,100	St. George and the Dragon
5. Polish American	1,000	The Atomic Cloud
6. Avalon	850	The Crusaders

	Winners	Prize Money	Theme
	7. Trilby	600	Musical Clowns
	8. Fralingers	400	Harvest Moon
	9. Fire-Fighters	300	Boys in Blue
	10. Hegeman	250	Moonlight over Niagara
	11. Uptown	200	Four Leaf Clover
	12. Uptown	150	Cadets of 1947
	13. Broomall	100	Me and My Shadow
	14. South Philadelphia	50	Egyptians

OH DEM
GOLDEN
SLIPPERS

Captain's Prizes

	Winners	Prize Money	Theme
	1. Joseph A. Ferko	75	Ferko String Band
	2. Walter Krop	50	Polish American String Band
	3. Harry Lawson	25	Avalon String Band

1948

	Winners	Prize Money	Theme
	1. Durning	1,375	Peg O'My Heart
	2. Ferko	1,275	Redwing Revelers
	3. Quaker City	1,175	King of the Aztecs
	4. Aqua	1,075	The Horn of Plenty
	5. Polish American	975	Peace for the World
	6. Fralinger	825	Auld Lang Syne
	7. Hegeman	575	Lucky Stars
	8. Greater Kensington	375	16th-Century Frenchmen
	9. Broomall	275	Sun Valley Serenade
	10. Avalon	225	Musical Fantasy
	11. Woodland	175	The Moth and the Flame
	12. South Philadelphia	175	Dutch Boys
	13. Fire-Fighters	100	Dixie Minstrels
	14. Trilby	100	Rocketmen
	15. Uptown	100	Philadelphia on Parade
	16. Northeast	100	Hearts
	17. Delaware County	100	Freshmen Year

Captain's Prizes

	Winners	Prize Money	Theme
	1. Walter Krop	25	Polish American String Band
	2. Raymond Endriss	15	Quaker City String Band
	3. Fred J. Kesel	10	Aqua String Band

1949

	Winners	Prize Money	Theme
	1. Polish American	1,100	Every Cloud Has a Silver Lining
	2. Ferko	1,000	Dancing Daisies
	3. Durning	900	Golden Slippers
	4. Quaker City	800	Blue Shadows on the Trail
	5. Hegeman	700	The Down of a New Day
	6. Woodland	600	Roses of Picardy
	7. Aqua	550	Mummers Parasols
	8. Fire-Fighters	500	Twilight Time
	9. Greater Kensington	450	Out of This World
	10. Fralinger	400	Men of Atlantis
	11. Trilby	350	King Momus
	12. Uptown	325	Glorified Clovers
	13. Garden State	300	Say It With Music
	14. Broomall	275	Neptune's Royal Guards
	15. Avalon	250	The Maharajah of Magidor
	16. Ukrainian American	225	Musical Graduates
	17. Delaware County	200	The Prince of India

176

Non-Prize Winners

	Winners		Theme
	Dick Crean		Rainbow Warriors
	McDall Post		Painting the Clouds with Sunshine

	Winners	Prize Money	Theme
	Northeast		America
	Palmyra		Hindustan
	South Jersey		Gay Ranchero
	South Philadelphia		Snow Crystals
	Whitman		Super Sonic Strings

Captain's Prizes

1.	Walter Krop	35	Polish American String Band
2.	Joseph A. Ferko	25	Ferko String Band
3.	Alfred E. Fink	15	Hegeman String Band

1950

1.	Ferko	1,650	Milady's Fan
2.	Polish American	1,550	The Pyramid and the Sphinx
3.	Quaker City	1,450	Stout Hearted Men
4.	Woodland	1,350	Dreamland
5.	Durning	1,250	The Crusaders
6.	Greater Kensington	1,110	Show Boat
7.	Fralinger	1,000	Musical Tribute to Stephen Foster
8.	Fire-Fighters	900	Tulip Time
9.	Hegeman	800	Candle-Light Time
10.	Aqua	700	Merry-Go-Round
11.	Garden State	600	Tulip Time in Holland
12.	Broomall	500	South American Way
13.	Ukrainian American	450	Apple Blossom Time
14.	Uptown	350	Fan-C-Melody
15.	Avalon	300	Blue and Broken Hearted
16.	Harrowgate	250	Royal Men of Egypt
17.	South Philadelphia	200	All Dressed Up with a Broken Heart

Non Prize Winners

	Dick Crean		Orchids Under Stars
	Delaware County		Grand Finale, Minstrel Time
	Frankford		Huckleberry Finn
	Mayfair		Clowns
	Palmyra		Sultan and Entourage
	South Jersey		The King and His Men
	Trilby		Tropicano, U.S.A.
	Whitman		Volunteer Firemen of Yesteryear

Captain's Prizes

1.	Alfred E. Fink	125	Hegeman String Band
2.	George Duffy	100	Fire-Fighters String Band
3.	Walter Krop	50	Polish American String Band
4.	Fred J. Kesel	25	Aqua String Band

1951

1.	Ferko	1,650	A Holiday at the Corral
2.	Uptown	1,550	Our American Heritage
3.	Durning	1,450	Pirates of Penzance
4.	Aqua	1,350	Nubian Slaves
5.	Hegeman	1,250	Minute Men for the World
6.	Duffy	1,150	Glorified Jockies
7.	Polish American	1,050	The Fountain of Youth
8.	Greater Kensington	900	The Road to Mandalay
9.	Fralinger	800	A Pretty Girl Is Like a Melody
10.	Woodland	700	Stars Are the Windows of Heaven

APPENDIX

177

	Winners	Prize Money	Theme
OH DEM GOLDEN SLIPPERS	11. South Philadelphia	600	Poor Butterfly
	12. Quaker City	500	Songs of the Islands
	13. Avalon	450	Treasure Island
	14. Trilby	400	Penn's Treaty with the Indians
	15. Broomall	350	Winter Wonderland
	16. Whitman	300	Stars Are the Windows of Heaven
	17. Penndel	150	Does Your Heart Beat for Me
	18. Palmyra	100	Winter Wonderland
	19. Ukrainian American	70	Wedding in January
	20. Dick Crean	50	Farmers
	21. Mayfair	40	The Beach of Wacki, Wacki
	22. Harrowgate	35	Symbols of Ireland
	23. Delaware County	30	Troubadors of Peace
	24. Garden State	25	Marines

Captain's Prizes

	1. Fred J. Kesel	25	Aqua String Band
	2. Robert Runkle	15	Uptown String Band
	3. Howard Peoples	10	Greater Kensington String Band

1952

1. Polish American	1,900	Cameos from My Sweetheart
2. Ferko	1,750	Playing Cards
2. Trilby	1,750	Blue Champagne
4. Hegeman	1,550	Hail to the Sun
4. Uptown	1,550	Little Dutch Boy and Little Dutch Girl
6. Fralinger	1,400	Parade of the Wooden Soldiers
7. Quaker City	1,300	Bengal Lancers
8. Durning	1,150	American Crusaders
9. Woodland	1,050	Bluebird of Happiness
10. Aqua	950	Forest Pixies
11. Greater Kensington	850	Old Soldiers Never Die
12. South Philadelphia	750	Yankee Doodle Dandies
13. Whitman	700	Orchids in the Moonlight
14. Duffy	650	The Musical Clowns
15. Avalon	600	Sheik of Araby
16. Broomall	500	A Night in Venice
17. Greater Philadelphia	300	Fiesta
18. Ukrainian American	200	Wooden Soldiers
19. Dick Crean	150	Stars and Stripes Forever
20. Mayfair	100	Lady of Spain
21. Harrowgate	100	Red Sails in the Sunset

Non Prize Winners

Garden State		Space Cadets
Tinicum		Old Melodies
Palmyra		Bowery Dancers
Penndel		Glorified Cavaliers

Captain's Prizes

1. Walter Krop	50	Polish American String Band
2. Adam Quaglia	30	Trilby String Band
3. Alfred E. Fink	20	Hegeman String Band

1953

1. Hegeman	1,900	The Bells of Erin
2. Ferko	1,800	Musical Gems

178

Winners	Prize Money	Theme
3. Uptown	1,700	Glorified Butterflies
4. Dick Crean	1,600	The Wheel of Fortune
5. Polish American	1,500	The Vagabond King
6. Quaker City	1,400	The Sun and the Moon
7. Greater Kensington	1,300	The Gypsy Trail
8. Aqua	1,150	Fiesta
9. Avalon	1,050	Bouquet of Roses
10. Trilby	950	The Hit Parade
11. Fralinger	850	Charmaine and Royal Escort
12. South Philadelphia	800	Toreadors
13. Woodland	750	By the Sea
14. Durning	700	The Sheik of Araby
15. Broomall	650	Autumn Serenade
16. Greater Overbrook	600	The Top Hatters
17. Harrowgate	350	Heart of a Clown
18. Ukrainian American	250	Down Mummery Lane

Non Philadelphia Bands

19. Penndel	600	Planets of Celeste
20. Palmyra	500	Rainbows Round My Shoulder
21. Garden State	400	Holiday for Strings
22. Tinicum	300	Stars in Your Eyes

Captain's Prizes

1. Charles Bremser	50	Dick Crean String Band
2. Robert Runkle	30	Uptown String Band
3. Alfred E. Fink	20	Hegeman String Band

1954

1. Polish American	2,000	The Mexican Hat Dance
2. Ferko	1,900	Apple Blossoms
3. Hegeman	1,800	The Sultan and Sabre
4. Avalon	1,700	The Artists from Moulin Rouge
5. Woodland	1,550	Princes of Music
6. Uptown	1,450	Out of the Deep Blue Sea
7. Quaker City	1,400	Alabama Jubilee
8. Broomall	1,300	Banjoes on Parade
9. Fralinger	1,250	An Eddie Cantor Revue
10. Greater Kensington	1,200	An Old Fashioned Garden
11. Aqua	1,100	The Bird in the Gilded Cage
12. Dick Crean	950	Welcome Hawaii
12. Garden State	950	The Wishing Well
14. South Philadelphia	850	A Mummer's Dream
15. Trilby	700	Eskimo and the Northern Lights
16. Crescentville	600	The Wizard of Oz
17. Ukrainian American	500	Candy
18. Durning	400	The Bells of St. Mary's
19. Greater Overbrook	275	The Knight of the Rose
19. Palmyra	275	The Gypsy Caravan
21. Harrowgate	200	Oklahoma Sunburst
22. Greater Bucks County	150	Erin Go Braugh

Captain's Prizes

1. Joseph A. Ferko	150	Ferko String Band
2. Walter Krop	100	Polish American String Band
3. Alfred E. Fink	50	Hegeman String Band

	Winners	Prize Money	Themes
	1955		
OH DEM	1. Polish American	2,000	Can Can
	2. Greater Kensington	1,900	Highlanders
GOLDEN	3. Dick Crean	1,800	Sunrise
SLIPPERS	4. Quaker City	1,700	Show Business
	5. Hegeman	1,600	The Ritual Dance of Fire
	6. Aqua	1,500	Siamese Dancers
	7. Uptown	1,400	Uptown on Parade
	8. Garden State1	1,300	Weather Vanes
	9. Ferko	1,250	The Student Prince
	10. Durning	1,175	Wooden Soldiers
	10. Trilby	1,175	Pennies from Heaven
	12. Crescentville	1,050	The Serenade of the Bells
	13. Greater Overbrook	950	Vineyard
	14. Woodland	850	Somewhere Over the Rainbow
	15. Fralinger	700	The Student Prince
	16. Broomall	600	Dixie
	17. Greater Bucks County	500	Sweethearts on Parade
	18. South Philadelphia	350	Melodies of the Golden West
	18. Avalon	350	Mr. Sandman
	20. Harrowgate	250	Garden of Roses
	21. Palmyra	200	Lady of Spain

Captain's Prizes

	Winners	Prize Money	Themes
	1. Fred J. Kesel	250	Aqua String Band
	2. Walter Krop	200	Polish American String Band
	3. James King	150	Garden State String Band
	1956		
	1. Quaker City	2,000	White Cloud
	2. Hegeman	1,900	George M. Cohan
	3. Uptown	1,800	Black Magic
	4. Ferko	1,650	Birds of Paradise
	4. Polish American	1,650	Ballroom Scene from the Merry Widow Waltz
	6. South Philadelphia	1,500	Harbor Lights
	7. Greater Kensington	1,400	Snow White and the Seven Dwarfs
	8. Woodland	1,300	Blossom Time
	9. Aqua	1,250	Aqua-Cade
	10. Trilby	1,200	The Naughty Twenties
	11. Dick Crean	1,150	Autumn Leaves
	12. Broomall	1.050	An Irish Festival
	13. Greater Overbrook	950	American Indians
	14. Greater Bucks County	850	Turn Back the Hands of Time
	15. Fralinger	700	Blue and Broken Hearted
	16. Garden State	600	The Glen Miller Story
	17. Durning	500	Ridin' on a Rainbow
	18. Avalon	400	Texas
	19. Palmyra	300	An Oriental Serenade
	20. Harrowgate	250	Mummers March
180	21. Crescentville	200	Mambo Kings

Captain's Prizes

	Winners	Prize Money	Themes
	1. David Amderson, Jr.	250	Woodland String Band
	2. Fred J. Kesel	200	Aqua String Band
	3. Robert Runkle	150	Uptown String Band

Winners	Prize Money	Themes	
1957			
1. Uptown	2,000	Syncopated Clock	APPENDIX
2. Fralinger	1,900	My Blue Heaven	
3. Ferko	1,800	Southern Capers	
4. Hegeman	1,700	A Smile Will Go a Long, Long Way	
5. Polish American	1,600	Polka Time	
6. Avalon	1,500	Melody of Love	
7. Quaker City	1,400	Mardi-Gras	
8. Trilby	1,300	Garden in the Rain	
9. Woodland	1,250	Anniversary Waltz	
10. South Philadelphia	1,200	Stardust	
11. Dick Crean	1,150	Allegheny Moon	
12. Aqua	1,050	Heart of a Clown	
13. Greater Bucks County	950	Monocan Guards	
14. Greater Overbrook	850	A Show Boat Revue	
15. Garden State	700	Our Friendly Neighbors	
16. Ukrainian American	600	Gay Nineties	
17. Palmyra	500	Waiting for the Sunrise	
18. Harrowgate	400	Rainbow Fantasy	
19. Durning	300	American Beauties	
20. Broomall	250	The Great Locomotive	
21. Greater Kensington	200	Desert Guards	
22. Crescentville	150	Winter Wonderland	

Captain's Prizes

1. John J. Fralinger	250	Fralinger String Band	
2. Robert Runkle	150	Uptown String Band	
3. Walter Krop	100	Polish American String Band	

1958			
1. Ferko	2,100	My Fair Lady	
2. Quaker City	2,000	Under the Big Top	
3. Uptown	1,900	Carousel	
4. Polish American	1,750	Salute to the Nation	
4. South Philadelphia	1,750	Songs of Spring	
6. Aqua	1,600	This Is Show Business	
7. Greater Kensington	1,450	The Rodeo	
8. Hegeman	1,450	Around the World in 80 Days	
9. Fralinger	1,350	Dancing Chandeliers	
10. Greater Overbrook	1,300	The Tango	
11. Woodland	1,250	Rose Marie	
12. Avalon	1,150	My Wonderful One	
13. Greater Bucks County	1,050	Disneyland	
14. Duffy	950	Golden Jubilee	
15. Trilby	800	Glo-Worm	
16. Durning	700	The American Jockey	
17. Ukrainian American	600	Night and Day	181
18. Broomall	500	Mississippi Gambler	
19. Palmyra	400	Trip to Dreamland	
20. Dick Crean	350	A Tribute to the Dorsey Brothers	
21. Garden State	300	Christmas in Killarney	
22. Harrowgate	200	Snuffy Smith and His Feather Merchants	

	Winners	Prize Money	Themes

Captain's Prizes

Winners	Prize Money	Themes
1. James Donaghy	200	South Philadelphia String Band
2. Fred J. Kesel	150	Aqua String Band
3. Robert Runkle	100	Uptown String Band

1959

Winners	Prize Money	Themes
1. South Philadelphia	2,100	African Fantasy
2. Polish American	2,000	Melodies of the Season
3. Greater Bucks County	1,900	The Great White Way
4. Ferko	1,800	Carnival of Venice
5. Fralinger	1,700	Toyland
6. Aqua	1,600	Gypsy Baron
7. Greater Kensington	1,500	King and I
8. Greater Overbrook	1,400	American Jubilee
9. Harrowgate	1,350	Prince of India
10. Hegeman	1,300	Cavalcade of States
11. Uptown	1,250	Puppets on Parade
12. Duffy	1,150	Serenade of the Stars
13. Garden State	1,050	The Cobra and the Charmer
14. Durning	950	An Orchid to You
15. Palmyra	800	Serenade of the Bells
16. Woodland	700	Easter Parade
17. Trilby	600	Honor Guard of the Mummers Hall of Fame
18. Quaker City	500	When Hearts Are Young
19. Avalon	400	Welcome Alaska
20. Broomall	350	Tournament of Roses
21. Ukrainian American	300	Prisoner of Love

Captain's Prizes

Winners	Prize Money	Themes
1. James Donaghy	250	South Philadelphia String Band
2. John J. Fralinger	175	Fralinger String Band
3. Frank Weller	125	Greater Bucks County String Band
4. James J. King	100	Garden State String Band

1960

Winners	Prize Money	Themes
1. Aqua	2,250	Tropicana Holiday
2. Polish American	2,150	Ziegfield Follies
3. Quaker City	2,050	Basin Street to Broad Street
4. Ferko	1,950	Musical Cavaliers
5. Greater Overbrook	1,850	Holiday in Paris
6. South Philadelphia	1,750	Lamps for Milady
7. Fralinger	1,650	My Island of Dreams
8. Uptown	1,550	Song Hits of Yesterday
8. Duffy	1,550	Swiss Festival
10. Durning	1,450	A Salute to Erin
11. Hegeman	1,400	Turkish Delight
12. Palmyra	1,300	Showboat
13. Greater Bucks County	1,200	Champagne Waltz
14. Woodland	1,100	Cherry Pink and Apple Blossom White
15. Harrowgate	950	Spain Comes to Mexico
16. Broomall	850	Isle of Golden Dreams
17. Trilby	750	Sacred Men of Buddha
18. Greater Kensington	650	The Gay Nineties
19. Garden State	550	Rock 'n' Roll
20. Avalon	500	An Irishman's Dream

Winners	Prize Money	Themes
21. Ukrainian American	450	Happy Minstrels
22. Dick Crean	150	Mardi-Gras

Captain's Prizes

1. James Donaghy	300	South Philadelphia String Band
2. John J. Fralinger	200	Fralinger String Band
3. Fred Kesel	175	Aqua String Band
4. Walter Krop	150	Polish American String Band
5. Henry Kunzig	125	Duffy String Band
6. Adam Quaglia	100	Trilby String Band
7. Robert Runkle	50	Uptown String Band

1961

1. Polish American	2,150	Holiday in Scotland
2. Ferko	2,050	The Blue and the Gray
3. Aqua	1,950	Bravo Brasilia
4. Greater Overbrook	1,850	Swamp Fire
5. Fralinger	1,750	Mother
6. Hegeman	1,600	South Sea Warriors
7. Greater Kensington	1,500	Gentlemen, Be Seated
8. Garden State	1,400	Signs of the Zodiac
9. Greater Bucks County	1,350	Indian Fantasy
10. Duffy	1,300	A Pagan Goddess
11. Harrowgate	1,250	Chiefs of Oklahoma
12. Uptown	1,200	A Tournament of Roses
13. South Philadelphia	1,150	Treasure Island
14. Ukrainian American	1,100	Rainbow Showers
15. Quaker City	1,050	Fiesta Espanola
16. Palmyra	950	Stairway to the Stars
17. Woodland	850	The World Is Waiting for the Sunrise
18. Broomall	750	Philadelphia's Own Hall of Fame
19. Avalon	650	The Least Thanked
20. Durning	500	A Salute to Mr. Mummer
21. Trilby	400	Happy Day
22. Dick Crean	200	French Artists

Captain's Prizes

1. Walter Krop	200	Polish American String Band
2. Ralph Annello	150	Garden State String Band
3. Henry Kunzig	125	Duffy String Band
4. John J. Fralinger	100	Fralinger String Band
5. Fred J. Kesel	75	Aqua String Band

1962

1. Hegeman	2,150	King Momus and His Subjects
2. Polish American	2,050	Return of the Conquering Romans
3. Quaker City	1,950	McNamara's Band
4. Ferko	1,850	Egypt and the Nile
5. South Philadelphia	1,750	The King and I
6. Fralinger	1,600	The Little Big Horn
7. Aqua	1,500	Wagon Train
8. Uptown	1,400	Silver Jubilee—25 Years
9. Duffy	1,350	Carnival Magic
10. Greater Kensington	1,300	A Connecticut Yankee in King Arthur's Court
11. Palmyra	1,250	Days of the Kaleidoscope
12. Greater Overbrook	1,200	A Roman Holiday

183

	Winners	Prize Money	Theme
	13. Woodland	1,150	A Tribute to Stephen Foster
	14. Garden State	1,100	Michael the Archangel and Lucifer
	15. Greater Bucks County	1,050	Satan Takes a Holiday
	16. Avalon	950	Camelot
	17. Durning	850	Dreams
	18. Ukrainian American	750	Gobs and Music
	19. Trilby	650	A Night in Las Vegas
	20. Dick Crean	500	Salute to Alaska
	21. Broomall	400	Holiday in Rio
	22. Harrowgate	200	Wonderful 20's

Captain's Prizes

	Prize Money	
1. Ralph Annello	200	Garden State String Band
2. Henry Kunzig	150	Duffy String Band
3. Raymond Endriss	125	Quaker City String Band
4. Frank Weller	100	Greater Bucks County String Band
5. Adam Quaglia	75	Trilby String Band

1963

	Prize Money	Theme
1. Quaker City	2,340	Gypsy Tambourines
2. Polish American	2,240	The Geisha God and the Maidens
3. South Philadelphia	2,140	Let a Smile Be Your Umbrella
4. Hegeman	2,040	Ragtime Banjo Kings
5. Ferko	1,940	The Bowery
6. Greater Bucks County	1,840	Dixie Dans
7. Fralinger	1,740	John Philip Sousa, the March King
8. Ukrainian American	1,640	From Out of This World
9. Greater Kensington	1,540	Mexican Fiesta
10. Woodland	1,440	Aztec Warriors
11. Greater Overbrook	1,390	Square Dance Jamboree
12. Aqua	1,340	Hold That Tiger
13. Avalon	1,290	25th Anniversary
14. Broomall	1,240	The Pearly Kings of London
15. Garden State	1,190	Summertime in Venice
16. Uptown	1,140	Waltz Times
17. Duffy	1,040	Chapel Bells
18. Palmyra	990	Heartbreak
19. Dick Crean	890	Buffalo Bill, Wild West Show
20. Durning	740	Lady of Spain
21. Trilby	575	Maharajah and His Harem
22. Harrowgate	400	Spanish Bull Fight

Captain's Prizes

	Prize Money	
1. Richard Egert	100	Polish American String Band
2. James Donaghy	75	South Philadelphia String Band
3. Ralph Annello	50	Garden State String Band

1964

	Prize Money	Theme
1. Polish American	2,270	Fantasy of Jungle Drums
2. Greater Kensington	2,170	From Paris to You
3. South Philadelphia	2,070	Hail to the Redskins
4. Ferko	1,970	The Three Musketeers
5. Fralinger	1,870	Camptown Capers
6. Ukrainian American	1,770	Old Ukraine
7. Quaker City	1,670	The King & His Royal Jesters
8. Greater Bucks County	1,570	The Fighting 69th
9. Hegeman	1,470	Circus Fantastique
10. Garden State	1,370	Blessed Event
11. Woodland	1,320	Big Tiny Little & His Honky Tonk Revue

Winners	Prize Money	Theme
12. Trilby	1,270	Diamonds Are a Girl's Best Friend
13. Greater Overbrook	1,220	Cinderella
14. Aqua	1,170	Halftime
15. Duffy	1,120	Greek Erzones
16. Broomall	1,070	A Musical Tribute to Johnny Appleseed
17. Harrowgate	850	Garden of Roses
18. Dick Crean	670	Harvest Time
19. Uptown	525	Floral Design
20. Durning	350	Parade of the Wooden Soldiers

1965

Winners	Prize Money	Theme
1. Greater Bucks County	2,310	The Hawaiian War Chant
2. Ukrainian American	2,210	The Anointment of King Solomon
3. Ferko	2,110	Horn of Plenty
4. Greater Kensington	1,010	Walt Disney's Fantasy Land
5. Woodland	1,910	Florentine Festival
6. Garden State	1,810	Phantasmagoria
7. Polish American	1,710	What Price Glory
8. Aqua	1,610	The Year of the Dragon
9. Durning	1,510	Star of Israel
10. Quaker City	1,410	Minstrel Days
11. Hegeman	1,360	Irish Valentines
12. Fralinger	1,310	The Bull Fight
13. South Philadelphia	1,260	Dixie Land Goes to the Mardi Gras
14. Trilby	1,210	Hello Dolly
15. Duffy	1,160	Dancing Rhythm
16. Greater Overbrook	1,110	Jimmy Schnozzle Durante
17. Uptown	1,010	Polynesian Fantasy
18. Dick Crean	960	Rags to Riches
19. Avalon	860	The Birth of a Nation
20. Broomall	710	The Cold Stream Guards

Captain's Prizes

Winners	Prize Money	Theme
1. Frank Weller	125	Greater Bucks County String Band
2. Ed Venckus	100	Aqua String Band
3. Phil Lipiecki	75	Polish American String Band

1966

Winners	Prize Money	Theme
1. South Philadelphia	2,270	String Band Hit Parade
2. Polish American	2,170	Brazilian Carnival
3. Aqua	2,070	Lithuania
4. Greater Bucks County	1,970	Tribute to Emmet Kelley
5. Greater Kensington	1,870	The Vanishing American
6. Ferko	1,770	Bengal Lancers
7. Broomall	1,670	Pussy Cats on Parade
8. Trilby	1,570	Dancing Sea Shells
9. Durning	1,470	Calendar Girl
10. Woodland	1,370	The Grand Revue of the Folies Bergere
11. Fralinger	1,320	Music Man
12. Quaker City	1,270	Prince of India
13. Greater Overbrook	1,220	Birds of a Feather
14. Harrowgate	1,170	A New Year Party
15. Hageman	1,120	A Walk in Space
16. Ukrainian American	1,070	Rebecca of Port Said
17. Dick Crean	970	Fraternal Order of Redmen

	Winners	Prize Money	Theme
	18. Garden State	920	Shangri La
OH DEM	19. Uptown	820	Stick to Uncle Sam
GOLDEN	20. Duffy	670	One Dozen Roses
SLIPPERS	21. Avalon	525	The Wizard of Oz
	22. Palmyra	350	No theme (17 members marched).

Captain's Prizes

1. James Donaghy	100	South Philadelphia String Band
2. Ed Venckus	75	Aqua String Band
3. Phil Lipiecki	50	Polish American String Band

1967

	Winners	Prize Money	Theme
1. Fralinger	2,470	The Magic of Toyland
2. Ferko	2,370	Jesters of Mirth and Melody
3. Woodland	2,270	Encore of Broadway Favorites
4. Polish American	2,170	The Lonely Bull
5. South Philadelphia	2,070	Chant of the Jungle
6. Greater Kensington	1,970	Manhattan Merry-Go-Round
7. Quaker City	1,870	Harvest Fantasy
8. Greater Overbrook	1,770	Mardi Gras
9. Hegeman	1,670	The Dixie Diamonds
10. Aqua	1,570	Holiday in Paris
11. Ukrainian American	1,520	The Gay Nineties
12. Trilby	1,470	Salute to the Emerald Isle
13. Greater Bucks County	1,420	Norseman
14. Garden State	1,370	Rhythmic Variations of the Eyes
15. Uptown	1,320	Mexican Fantasy
16. Harrowgate	1,270	Songs of the Desert
17. Durning	1,170	Calendar Girl
18. Duffy	1,120	A German Festival
19. Avalon	1,020	String Band Festival
20. Dick Crean	870	A Dutch Mill Serenade
21. Palmyra	725	Barber Shop Quartet on Parade
22. Broomall	550	A Tribute to Mame

Captain's Prizes

1. David Anderson	125	Woodland String Band
2. Ray Endriss	100	Quaker City String Band
3. Curtis V. Steur	75	Ferko String Band
4. John Fralinger	25	Fralinger String Band

1968

	Winners	Prize Money	Theme
1. Fralinger	2,470	The Bells of St. Mary's
2. Ferko	2,370	Tiajuana Fiesta
3. South Philadelphia	2,270	King of the Road
4. Greater Overbrook	2,170	Winter Wonderland
5. Aqua	2,070	Legend of the Aztecs
6. Woodland	1,970	Golden Memories of Mummery
7. Quaker City	1,870	The Merry Men of Sherwood
8. Polish American	1,770	Musical Follies of Guys & Gals
9. Greater Bucks County	1,670	Mikado
10. Trilby	1,570	Sun Worshippers
11. Uptown	1,520	Kabuki Lion Dancers
12. Greater Kensington	1,470	How the West Was Won
13. Garden State	1,420	Anatomy of a Storm
14. Hegeman	1,370	Aurora Borealis
15. Palmyra	1,320	Robin Hood
16. Harrowgate	1,270	South Rampart Street Parade
17. Ukrainian American	1,170	Prisoners of Love

Winners	Prize Money	Theme
18. Avalon	1,120	The Greatest Show on Earth
19. Duffy	1,020	Roman Festival
20. Durning	870	Sounds of the Times
21. Dick Crean	725	The Mummers Strut at Quebec's Joyeux Carnival
22. Broomall	550	Blue Champagne

Captain's Prizes

1. Ed Venckus	125	Aqua String Band
2. Curtis V. Steur, Sr.	100	Ferko String Band
3. John J. Fralinger	75	Fralinger String Band
4. James Donaghy	25	South Philadelphia String Band

1969

1. Ferko	2,470	Show Girls of Great Shows
2. Polish American	2,370	A Nubian Tribute to the Pharaoh
3. Greater Kensington	2,270	As Time Goes By
4. Woodland	2,170	A Salute to George M. Cohan
5. Palmyra	2,070	A Salute to the Mummers
6. Fralinger	1,970	Let a Smile Be Your Umbrella
7. Quaker City	1,870	The Wizards of Love
8. South Philadelphia	1,770	Songs of the Islands
9. Greater Overbrook	1,670	Caribbean Holiday
10. Garden State	1,570	Kite Fantasia
11. Hegeman	1,152	Springtime in Old Paree
12. Harrowgate	1,470	Storybook Fantasy
13. Duffy	1,420	The Gingerbread Men
14. Durning	1,370	Moonlight Melodies
15. Aqua	1,320	Everything Is Coming up Roses
16. Greater Bucks County	1,270	The Pennsylvania Dutch
17. Broomall	1,170	Let Freedom Ring
18. Uptown	1,120	Say It with Music
19. Avalon	1,020	This Land is Your Land and Mine
20. Ukrainian American	870	Is Everybody Happy?
21. Dick Crean	725	Collegiate 1930
22. Trilby	550	Butterfly Fantasy

Captain's Prizes

1. Ralph Annello	125	Garden State String Band
2. Mickey Mallon	100	Greater Kensington String Band
3. David Anderson	75	Woodland String Band
4. Phil Lipiecki	25	Polish American String Band

1970

1. Polish American	2,470	Showtime Internationale
2. Hegeman	2,370	Through the Years with the Hegeman String Band
3. Fralinger	2,270	Italian Melodies, Old and New
4. Aqua	2,170	Cherry Pink and Apple Blossom White
5. Ferko	2,070	Aladdin's Lucky Day
6. Quaker City	1,970	Hello Sunshine, Good-bye Rain
7. Woodland	1,870	An Old Fashioned Wedding
8. Trilby	1,770	The Golden Slipper
9. Greater Overbrook	1,670	A Salute to Jimmy Durante
10. Garden State	1,570	Fountain of Youth
11. Greater Kensington	1,520	Sunrise, Sunset
12. Uptown	1,470	The Melodious Merrymakers

	Winners	Prize Money	Theme
OH DEM GOLDEN SLIPPERS	13. Harrowgate	1,420	Casey Jones
	14. South Philadelphia	1,370	There's a Rainbow 'Round My Shoulder
	15. Durning	1,320	Oriental Holiday
	16. Ukrainian American	1,270	Hippies
	17. Avalon	1,170	Happy Music
	18. Palmyra	1,120	Over There
	19. Duffy	1,020	Age of Aquarius
	20. Greater Bucks County	870	Rainbow Clowns
	21. Dick Crean	725	Sunshine of Happiness
	22. Broomall	550	Sun Valley Serenade

Captain's Prizes

1. Mickey Mallon	125	Greater Kensington String Band
2. Anthony Bordoni	100	Uptown String Band
3. Dave Myers	75	Harrowgate String Band
4. Ed Venckus	25	Aqua String Band

MUMMERS' HALL OF FAME

1956	Harry Roberts	Jack Towers	David W. Crawford
1957	George B. McClernand	Joseph A. Ferko	Henry Saltenberger
1958	Harry Tyler	James A. Durning	James McGlinchy
1959	Joseph Purul	Fred J. Kesel	John J. Lawler
1960	Billie Torelli	Peter A. Broomall	Joseph Napoleon
1961	Jack Carlo	Raymond Endriss	S. D. Wheeler
1962	John Gallaway	Robert Runkle, Jr.	Charles Dumont, Sr.
1963	Philip J. Hammond	Raymond Gurt	John J. Hines
1964	Joseph Schultz	Walter Krop	James Kinee
1965	Raymond Bordier	Harry Straub	Harry Jerdon
1966	Henry Leh	Harry Lawson	Harry F. Marquis, Sr.
1967	Nicholas Matteo	William Mink	Henry Hendrickson
	Frank Iacuzio	Harry Whitman	George Horshaft
1968	Joseph Hammond	John Fralinger	Ralph Tursi
	I. Reds Ramsay	David Anderson	Andrew Sheridan
1969	Dommie Torelli	Robert Hall	William Isaacs, Sr.
	Frank Stermel	John Hogg	Rudy Meech

PEPPER POT SOUP

Here is Christopher Bastian's recipe, the same as it was 150 years ago except that with a pre-cooked variety of tripe now available, cooking time is cut by some 5 hours. The basic recipe serves 6.

5 lbs. pre-cooked tripe	salt	2 cups flour
5 medium sized potatoes	pepper	2 eggs
1 onion	marjoram	2 tsp. of baking pdr.
3 quarts water	pot herbs	2/3 cup milk

Cut pre-cooked tripe into medium sized chunks and place in boiling water. Add veal knuckle, salt, pepper, to taste and cook for 1½ hours. Remove tripe and knuckle bone. Dice tripe in 1 inch pieces and return to broth. Add diced raw potatoes, finely chopped onion. Add bunch of pot herbs and generous pinch of marjoram. Cook ½ hour. Mix flour, beaten eggs, baking powder and milk into a batter and drop into the boiling broth a tablespoonful at a time for drop dumplings. Serve hot.

Taken from Julie Frey, "On Pepper Pot," *Greater Philadelphia Magazine*, February, 1954, p. 10.

INDEX

Oh, dem Golden Slippers.